IMAGES
of America

THREE TREE POINT

This southerly view of Three Tree Point shows a portion of its 2.5 miles of waterfront extending into Puget Sound with Mount Rainier in the background. (Author's collection.)

ON THE COVER: Passengers in their Sunday best are arriving at Three Tree Point from the steamer *Vashon* in 1910. The 94-foot vessel ran between Tacoma and Seattle, ferrying passengers to summer homes and campsites in the early days of Three Tree Point. The steamer was operated by Capt. Chauncey "Chance" Wiman and his wife, Gertrude, who in 1907 became the first woman on Puget Sound to obtain a second-class pilot's license. (Author's collection.)

IMAGES
of America

THREE TREE POINT

Doug Shadel, Pam Harper,
and Guy Harper

ARCADIA
PUBLISHING

Copyright © 2010 by Doug Shadel, Pam Harper, and Guy Harper
ISBN 978-1-5316-5314-9

Published by Arcadia Publishing
Charleston, South Carolina

Library of Congress Control Number: 2009937657

For all general information contact Arcadia Publishing at:
Telephone 843-853-2070
Fax 843-853-0044
E-mail sales@arcadiapublishing.com
For customer service and orders:
Toll-Free 1-888-313-2665

Visit us on the Internet at www.arcadiapublishing.com

*To all the marvelous residents of Three Tree
Point, past, present, and future.*

CONTENTS

ACKNOWLEDGMENTS

Photographs and data are from numerous sources: basements, attics, family albums, and the generous assistance of corporations, museums, and archives. If images are not credited, they are from the authors' collections.

This book would not have been possible without the photographs and memories provided by the residents of Three Tree Point. Those people who provided photographs, participated in interviews, or otherwise assisted with the creation of the book include Helen Anderson and Frank Anderson; Joan Anderson; Kathy and Todd Anderson; Walter Blair; Margaret Boyle; Robert Burgess; Michael Brunk; Tor Burkhard; Lynn Castillo; Melinda Catalano; Lynn and Ralph Davis; Gilbert Duffy; Wende Duffy; William Ellsworth; Anne and Fred Feiretag; Phil Fleming; Charles Ganong; Jerry Gay; Mary Ellen Conrad Gettmann; Lance Haslund; Jeff Hogan; Ethan Janson; Charles Johnson; Sue Korbet; Susan Kraft; Arden Leffler; Stan Lemmel; Laverne McIntyre; Bud Melby; Lonnie Miller; Sandra Sander Noreen; Page Palmer; Ken Pearson; Gordon Peek; Virginia Pearce; Lance Puckett; Michael Purcell; Greg Rehmke; Jonete Rehmke; Richard Rehmke; Ray Rice; Jerry Robinson; Andrew Ryan; Renee, Emily, and Nick Shadel; Morey Skaret; Florence Smallwood; Norton Smallwood Jr.; Peggy Steele; Sallie Holderness Tostberg; Thomas Verd; Diane Radinsky Wall; David and Mary Williams; Nancy Wilson; David Wintermute; and Gregory Worthing.

The following corporations and organizations were also very generous with their photographs and their historical expertise: the Duwamish Tribe; Kathrine Young at the Naval Undersea Museum, Navy Region Northwest; University of Washington Libraries, Special Collections Division; Carolyn Marr at the Museum of History and Industry; Phil Stairs at Washington State Archives, Puget Sound Regional Branch; Mary Kane at The Boeing Company; Karl House at the Puget Sound Maritime Historical Society; Highline Historical Society; Michael Skalley at Foss Maritime; National Records and Archives Administration, Naval Historical Foundation, Pacific Alaska Region; Three Tree Point Garden Club; Michael at NW Lens; and Maury Floathe at ION Corporation.

Publications used were *Scenes and Views at Three Tree Point*; *H. W. McCurdy Marine History of the Pacific Northwest*; *Steamers Wake* by Jim Faber; Scott Schaeffer at www.b-townblog.com; www.dcsfilms.com; www.historylink.org; www.newspaperarchives.org; Dale Miller at *Pacific Yachting*; *Marine Digest*; the *Highline Times*; Evelyn Edens at the *Seattle Times*; and the *New York Times*.

The authors have made a concerted effort to establish the veracity of the captions and chapter introductions, and they apologize for any errors the reader may find. Additionally, there were almost 300 photographs that the authors were not able to include due to space requirements.

INTRODUCTION

Along the eastern edge of Washington's Puget Sound, halfway between Seattle and Tacoma and within the city of Burien, lies a place made of equal parts myth, magic, and mystery. Its heritage is as rich and varied as the thousands of people who have combed its shores, plied its waters, and probed its headlands through the ages. Its magic still sparkles in names such as Maplewild, Crescent Beach, and the Moonlight Trail and in the lightly veiled mystery of why so many have become permanently attached to this prominent point of land. Much like drifting barnacles, they anchor themselves and never leave.

This place has many faces. Here sun, wind, sky, mountains, sand, and sea seamlessly coalesce into a living mosaic unchanged for millennia. True, the elements can be brutal, whether as icy north winds, pounding sou'westers, or monster waves clawing at the point's very backbone. But in her gentler moods, nature shimmers here like nowhere else, unfurling panoramic vistas, dazzling sunsets, and stunning seascapes.

This place has had many names, most of them lost in the mists of time: ai-YAH-hus (the abode of a huge snakelike creature), sx'elab ("a load"), t'aleyAqW (two canoes lashed together), kaka'alqo ("crow's water"), Point Pully (after Robert Pully, a member of the 1841 Wilkes Expedition), Lone Tree Point (after the fort built here in 1856, the name remaining on later King County maps), and finally Three Tree Point, officially designated as such in 1975, cementing its popular name.

This place, long a traditional site of human gathering, has had many residents—some permanent, others temporary. Native Americans—Duwamish, Muckleshoot, and other tribes—likely camped here, drawn by its rich fishing, clamming, and berry-picking grounds. With its geographical prominence, central-sound location, nearby freshwater springs, and sheltering bays, Three Tree Point would have made a natural rest stop on long canoe trips and perhaps a final resting place as well. Legend has it that the Native American dead were buried here beneath the small rise a stone's throw east of the point itself.

This place was strategically important as well. The high bluffs above the water offered unrestricted views up and down the sound and a perfect vantage point for detecting raiding parties of Tlingit, Haida, and other warlike tribes. Word of impending attack could be quickly spread to other lowland camps and villages, allowing those in harm's way to flee inland.

The first European to see Three Tree Point, sailing into Puget Sound in 1792 in search of the elusive Northwest Passage, was probably British naval captain George Vancouver. Vancouver noticed thick clouds of smoke blanketing the prominent finger of land, as the Indians often set fire to the surrounding forest to drive out game and create open spaces for foot travel and edible berries.

Thirty-two years would pass before the next European visitors laid eyes on Three Tree Point. In 1824, a 40-man expedition led by James McMillan of the Hudson's Bay Company sought a passage for small boats between the Columbia and Fraser Rivers. Traveling south through Puget Sound, they were driven ashore by rough weather and spent the evening of December 23, 1824, camped at the point.

By the 1850s, Puget Sound had become a key trade route and destination for settlers, leading to tensions and even war with the local Native American tribes. In 1856, Pierce County militia volunteers built Fort Lone Tree Point on or near Three Tree Point. Housing 10 to 20 men, the fort was intended to block Indian warriors' access to the area's converging trails. No warriors were ever detected in the area, however, during the War of 1855–1856.

American settlers, buoyed by the Homestead Act of 1862, began filing claims for large tracts of land around Three Tree Point. James and Robert Howe, for example, claimed 120 and 160 acres each, including most of the shoreline north and south of the point. Others followed suit.

But for decades the area remained isolated—at least by land—because the roads linking it to the outside were primitive at best and nearly impassable due to steepness, ruts, and mud. Luckily the Puget Sound "water highway" provided an easier means of traveling throughout the region well into the 20th century.

Dubbed the "Mosquito Fleet" due to its large number of vessels, a fleet of steamboats—supplemented by an odd mix of canoes, schooners, and other seaworthy craft—reliably ferried passengers, freight, and mail between Seattle and Tacoma. Three Tree Point was included as a port of call in the late 19th century, when burgeoning population growth gave a healthy boost to Puget Sound's steamship trade.

By the 1890s, as Three Tree Point became prime vacation property, even more boat service was needed. The McDowell Transportation Company, begun in 1898 and using seven boats, enjoyed a thriving business as more people flocked to summer resorts at Three Tree Point. In its heyday, the Mosquito Fleet made eight stops a day at the point, from 6:00 a.m. to 10:00 p.m.

By the early 1900s, more well-to-do Seattleites were building summer homes on the beaches north and south of Three Tree Point. There was one general store—as allowed by the deed restrictions imposed by the Seacoma Company, then owners of Three Tree Point—as well as a dock, vacation cottages, and pavilion and picnic grounds. Still, the only practical way to get here remained by water, with foot trails leading up from the dock through the forest.

By 1918, better roads and more automobiles finally spelled the decline of boat service to Three Tree Point and the end of the Mosquito Fleet in general. Although the Virginia steamships operated between Seattle and Tacoma for many years, stops at Three Tree Point were eliminated. Still, getting to Three Tree Point by land remained a challenge. The roads and trails winding down to the water from the end of the trolley line, at Southwest 152nd Street and Twenty-first Avenue Southwest in Seahurst, were treacherous. An alternate route opened about 1919 when Sylvester Road was cut through from Five Corners.

Three Tree Point's accessibility by water was especially convenient during Prohibition, when Canadian bootleggers used its darkened docks to smuggle in liquor. Apparently the smugglers, who stored their wares in a nearby basement, enjoyed the protection of local police—at least until federal authorities got wind of the operation.

The winds and waters off Three Tree Point haven't always been so benign, conspiring to produce several calamities over the years: ships running aground, capsizing, flipping over, or sinking; plane crashes; spectacular house fires lighting up the night sky for miles; and other perils. Yet the point's residents remain a hearty, humorous, and colorful group. You will meet them—the lives they led, the homes they built, the fun they had, and the world they made—in the following pages.

Today Three Tree Point offers beachcombing, windsurfing, swimming, waterskiing and jet skiing, kayaking, canoeing, fishing, scuba diving, and sailing. The Three Tree Point Yacht Club, formed in 1969, hosts year-round sailing events. North of the point, near the site of the old steamship dock, a 130-foot drop-off and rich array of sea life offer an enticing realm for divers. And the point's Fourth of July celebration includes parades by land and sea, activities for kids of all ages, and a spectacular fireworks display.

The authors hope that the pictures and words that follow accurately and colorfully capture the people, history, essence, and spirit of this unique community and convey a hint of the magic that surrounds Three Tree Point. So come on in, pull up a chair, and stay awhile, but be careful—you may never want to leave.

—Charles Ganong

One

THE EARLY YEARS

No one who visits this spot can leave without exclaiming, "Is it not dropped from heaven!"
There is a healing power in every breeze that bears upon its bosom the breath of pure sea air
and the sweet scent of the pines. Consider not your books and pens, my friends; for a little
while, put away anxious thoughts and the cares which corrode the soul, the responsibilities
of life and all concern therein; forget the money machine, the office and the workshop, the
daily task, whatever it may be, and go with me to the woods and the murmuring sea.

—*Scenes and Views at Three Tree Point*

In the summertime, native peoples came to Three Tree Point from their villages along the Duwamish River and Elliott Bay. They came by trail or canoe, attracted by the freshwater springs and the abundant food sources. There is no evidence that the Duwamish people lived at the point throughout the year. For them it was a summer retreat, a place to meet friends and to stock up for the winter.

The potential for development was recognized in the 1800s. James and Robert Howe, Bailey Gatzert, and the Schwabacher brothers were among the first to acquire land at Three Tree Point.

Platting of properties at the point began with the formation of the Three Tree Point Company. This enterprise was founded by pioneer Seattle businessmen James D. Lowman and Bernard Pelly and was managed by Charles B. Livermore. In 1902, the company purchased 267 acres of land that included 2.5 miles of waterfront. They began to prepare the land for real estate development.

For the next year, the company built wooden boardwalks, primitive roads, and trails; platted lots; and constructed park areas for picnicking. Beginning in July 1903, the company launched an aggressive marketing campaign to attract visitors and potential homeowners to the point. Unless otherwise noted, images in this chapter are taken from *Scenes and Views at Three Tree Point*, produced by the company in 1905.

Members of the Duwamish tribe traveled by canoe to Three Tree Point from their villages on Elliott Bay and further inland. By 1913, when Edward Curtis took this photograph, such modes of travel were seldom seen. Curtis wanted to document the traditional life of the native people before it disappeared. The image is from a collection of his photographs on display in the hallways, dining room, and meeting rooms of the Rainier Club in Seattle. (ION Corporation.)

When Native American and early explorers approached Three Tree Point from the north, this would have been their view. The long, flat point jutting out into Puget Sound is visible from West Point beyond Elliot Bay and from Poverty Bay near Redondo. The first home was built by Linden Irwell Gregory, a native of Lancashire, England, about 1902 and is probably the one that is visible in this photograph. (Gordon Peek.)

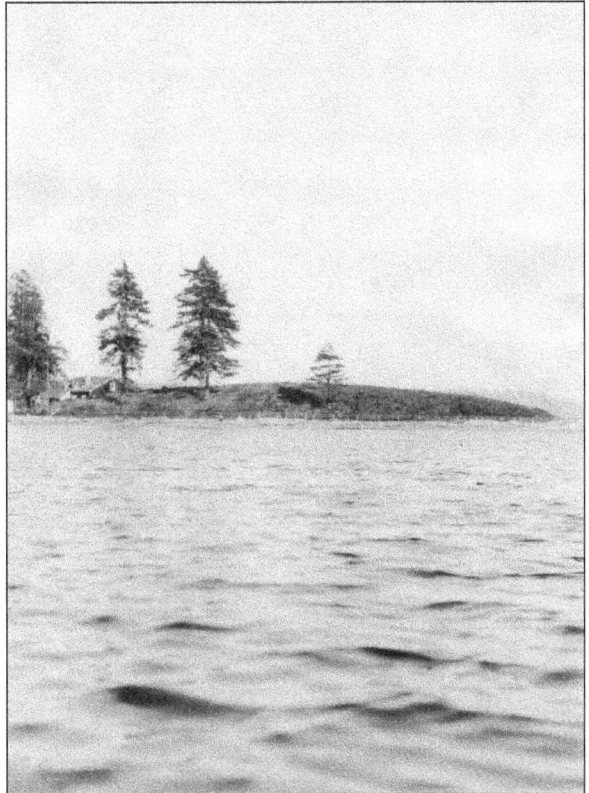

High tides and storms filled two saltwater lagoons in a low area just inside the point. The larger of the two had a circumference of 1,800 feet. Looking across the lagoon from the south, one can see a mound that Native Americans may have used as a burial ground. The prominent trees could be the ones that gave the point its name.

Beyond this view of the lagoon is a road going along the north side of the point, and by 1905 it was 20 feet wide. The lagoon was later filled with sand from a quarry at the east end of 171st Street. This part of the street is high above the point, and the sand was moved down the hill by means of a metal flume.

The Moonlight Trail was on the south side of the point. Erma Verd wrote that her father hired a horse and buggy and drove to Miller's Beach (now in Normandy Park) where the horse was left at a farm. Then they walked along this trail to Three Tree Point. Their arms would be loaded with baskets of food, clothes, and even a turkey at Thanksgiving. Part of the trail is still used today and runs between the lots along the beach and those on the bluff.

The Sunlight Trail on the north side was the only way for many property owners to reach their camps and cabins after they arrived at the dock. It was also used for hiking and provided wonderful views of the water. The photograph shows survey stakes placed along this trail marking the six-foot right-of-way. This picture was taken sometime before 1905. These trails may have been in the same location as those used by the Native Americans and have been called Indian trails for nearly 100 years.

Bailey Gatzert and the Schwabacher brothers, Seattle business pioneers, were listed on the 1895 tax rolls as owning land on Three Tree Point. Gatzert was elected mayor of Seattle in 1875. Here he is shown with the Schwabacher family. Pictured from left to right are Babette (Schwabacher) and Bailey Gatzert, Bella and Abraham Schwabacher, Sarah and Louis Schwabacher, and Sigmund and Rose Schwabacher. (Museum of History and Industry.)

Gatzert led a thriving hardware and grocery business with the Schwabachers in the late 1800s in downtown Seattle, as depicted in this 1870 photograph showing horse-drawn carriages parked in front of their store. (University of Washington Libraries, Special Collections Division, JEW0232.)

James D. Lowman was born in Leitersburg, Maryland, in 1856. He moved to Seattle in 1877 at the invitation of his uncle Henry Yesler. Lowman was considered to be one of Seattle's best-known pioneers, having founded the Lowman and Hanford Stationary Company and serving on numerous corporate boards and as president of the Seattle Chamber of Commerce. He was one of the founders of the Three Tree Point Company that transformed the point into a prestigious summer community. (*A History of Seattle*, Frederic James Grant.)

Charles B. Livermore was born in Wisconsin in 1850. In the early 1880s, he moved to Walla Walla, Washington, where he became active in real estate ventures. In 1899, he moved to Seattle where he formed a business partnership with J. D. Lowman, president of the Three Tree Point Company. Livermore was responsible for marketing the land purchased by the company in 1902. (Melinda Catalano).

Three Tree Point
Summer Homes

Three Tree Point
Summer Homes

Three Tree Point
Summer Homes

THE Company owns two and one-half miles of water front which is platted into lots, each lot having a sixty-foot water front, running back from one hundred to three hundred feet deep. The streets are graded, trails are also graded through the grounds which are now open for summer homes and home campers.

The Company has a large pavilion one hundred and twenty feet in diameter, arranged so that it can be divided into four halls, each separate and apart from the other, if necessary, for small family parties.

The grounds are open for engagement for the use of excursion parties, picnics, etc., save and except on Sabbath days. No application for the use of the grounds on that day will be considered. It is the desire of the Company that the grounds shall be used exclusively for its resident patrons and their friends on Sabbath days.

Five-room tents nicely floored will be erected for the use of summer campers for Fifty Dollars for the season. Grounds can be rented and campers furnish their own outfit for Twenty-five Dollars for the season.

* * *

Watch the papers closely for the announcement of the picnic to be held at Three Tree Point on July 7th. It will be the grand opening day. For complete information of terms and rates for picnic parties, conventions, prices of lots, etc., address

THREE TREE POINT CO.
C. B. LIVERMORE, MGR.

625 FIRST AVENUE - - SEATTLE, WASHINGTON

One of the first display ads taken out by the Three Tree Point Company in the *Seattle Mail and Herald* on July 3, 1903, advertised the new community to the public. The *Seattle Mail and Herald* went out of business in 1905.

A 1905 photograph shows the newly constructed wooden boardwalk that made it easier for visitors to walk between the dock and the picnic area or campsites. Several tent structures have been erected at the edge of the lagoon.

This view of the north beach shows several visitors strolling along the boardwalk. Another sign of development is the tall flagpole with a large American flag on a knoll overlooking the beach. Visible in the background is a road coming down to the beach. This may have been the location of the street end where the new dock was to be built.

The new dock is seen in the distance with an improved boardwalk leading to it. The building at the head of the dock was probably a store and ticket office. By the time this picture was taken, there were several homes built farther along the beach, and it would have been a distinct advantage to walk the boardwalk instead of negotiating all the logs and debris. (Gordon Peek.)

In the early years, there were deer and small game in abundance, and this hunter is walking the boardwalk with his dog. The Three Tree Point Company had no restrictions regarding hunting, and there were no licenses or seasonal closures associated with the activity.

One of the Three Tree Point Company tents is used as a hunting camp. Its brochure stated, "You may see some of the herd of deer headed by a watchful buck. This herd has been here many years and are a feature of the place that the company has taken special pains to preserve." Nevertheless, hunting was allowed.

This little boy stands in front of one of the tents described by the Three Tree Point Company in promotional materials, "The Company will furnish tents for occupancy, 10x12, 10x16, 10x24, with good floors, five-foot walls and canvas partitions in them that can be arranged so as to make from two to four sleeping apartments for family use. They are warm and comfortable and afford perfect protection. The tents will be furnished of either size for the season at $50. Parties who have tents of their own and wish to put them up themselves, will be furnished ground room for ten dollars per month." (Florence Smallwood.)

The firs and cabin are reflected in the lagoon that the Three Tree Point Company described, "The water in them is always fresh, coming in with the high tide and retiring as it goes out. Its shallow depths make it perfectly safe for women and children, and the sun naturally warms the water. Nowhere on the sound are there such natural and perfect bathing places. If the wind is blowing from the north, bathe on the south side; if blowing from the south, then you have the north side."

In 1903, a large pavilion was built on the point. It was octagonal in shape and 120 feet in diameter and could be partitioned into separate compartments. There was a promenade around the exterior so that dancers would "have the full sweep of the floor." Curtains could be drawn to keep out the wind and rain. An advertisement in the *Seattle Mail and Herald* on July 3, 1903, described the pavilion's availability, "The grounds are open for engagement for the use of excursion parties, picnics, etc. save and except for the Sabbath days. No application for the use of the ground on that day will be considered."

The first dock was just inside the north side of the point; however, it was exposed to the prevailing south winds and strong currents near the end of the point. Additionally, the original dock was located near one of the lagoons, which made access difficult. This location and dock proved unsatisfactory, and a sturdier dock was built on the north beach at the foot of what is now 170th Street behind the Three Tree Point Store. The photograph above shows the original dock and a crude wooden walkway between a lagoon and the beach. In the photograph at left, Phillip Almon Stuart waits for one of the Mosquito Fleet boats on the old dock. The pavilion can be seen in the background. (Both Gordon Peek.)

A view from the north beach shows the propeller-driven *Arrow* at the old Three Tree Point dock. (Gordon Peek.)

The Sunlight Trail followed the shoreline from the Three Tree Point dock around the cove to this location on the north beach. Along the hillside, building lots were partitioned above and below the trail. Several springs brought freshwater down the hillside and out onto the beach. This was the source of drinking water for the early development. These springs are still there and are channeled into pipes that run underneath the houses. The Sunlight Trail, now called the Indian Trail, is still in existence.

Edward Thomas Verd (1868–1941) built one of the first homes at Three Tree Point. In the cover photograph, he is dressed in a white hat on the left. Verd was the president of the Bryant Lumber Company in Seattle, where the Fremont Bridge is now. He married Amy I. Frost, and they had two children: Erma, born 1898, and Wesley, born 1902. Erma's daughter still lives in the home built by her grandfather in 1904. (Thomas Verd and Peggy Steele.)

Alice (second to right) and Jesse Stuart (far right), two of the early landowners on the point, are shown here sometime between 1905 and 1913 on the porch of their cabin on the north side of the point. The log house in the background was replaced by a much bigger home in 1913. (Gordon Peek.)

The boat has already departed, and this view from the Stuart house shows visitors coming up the dock. Someone in the community had an automobile for taking people to their camps and cabins. Only passenger ferries called at this dock. (Gordon Peek.)

The 1909 photograph above was probably taken from a steamboat tied to the dock. The Verd and Stuart houses on the left are still there, as shown in the photograph below, which was taken 100 years later. These homes look much the same as they did when new and are owned and occupied by grandchildren of the original builders. The two houses nearer the dock were torn down and replaced in 1913 by the large home in the picture below. There is a street end and public beach where the dock once stood, and a sewer pumping facility has been built above the rock bulkhead. This location is very popular with scuba divers because of its easy access and the abundance of sea life.

In this 1909 photograph, it appears that the mound that was visible in earlier photographs is gone, and at least one of the lagoons has been filled in. The pavilion doesn't show in this picture but may be obscured by the trees. On the far right is the old dock, which was still used by small vessels. The boardwalk is no longer evident, probably washed away by storms. The 2009 photograph below of the same location shows the elegant homes that have been built in recent years. The house in the picture above is still there but can no longer be seen from the water.

This photograph was taken from a high point on the Duffy property by Asahel Curtis in the early 1920s. (Wende Duffy.)

Two

MAKING WAVES

Commercial vessels have always fascinated and delighted residents of Three Tree Point. From the earliest days of steamships and sternwheelers, through the days of the Puget Sound Navigation Company and up until the time of modern cargo carriers, ships passed several times a day. They bring waves to the beach—to the north beach if the ship is traveling south and to the south beach if traveling north. Small children delight in leaping over the waves, and older ones take their speedboats out to jump the wake. In the summer there is always a concern about pulling up the dinghy or canoe because, when the waves come, they could be swamped.

The rules of the Vessel Traffic Navigation System require ships to pass on the right of the buoys marking the mid-channel. There is a navigation buoy off the point, and northbound vessels must therefore pass closer to the shore. At the point, the beach rises abruptly and has caught many a sailor and ship. Additionally, there have been several instances of ships and tugs going aground at various spots along the beach. The point itself has a navigation light with a foghorn that can be heard throughout surrounding neighborhoods, especially on fall days.

This poem, *Someone's Coming*, by Arden Leffler echoes the experience of all who live at the point:

I hear some thumping
In a rhythmic beat.
It sounds like an army
With loud marching feet.
My old house is shaking
The windows a-rattle.
The army comes closer.
Prepare for a battle.
Then around the Point
Comes the cause of commotion.

It's a large tanker ship
With out-of-sync motion.
Half out of water
The prop is vibrating.
A half-empty hold,
We feel it gyrating.
Our peace will return
As the ship bangs away
Heading north to Seattle
And out of our bay.

In *Scenes and Views at Three Tree Point*, printed in 1905, the above boat was identified as the *Three Tree Point*. Included was a schedule for transportation service between Seattle and the point. In fact, the boat was actually the *W. E. Harrington*, seen below. For their brochure, the owners of the Three Tree Point Company used the photograph of the *W. E. Harrington* and rather crudely changed the name on the bow and the wheelhouse and added a figure standing on the bow. Note that the pictures are the same, including the background. The Merchant Vessels of the United States Registers of 1901 to 1914 do not show a vessel with the name *Three Tree Point*. However, the *W. E. Harrington* was used on the Seattle-Alki Point-Three Tree Point route. (Karl House, Puget Sound Maritime Historical Society.)

This photograph from *Scenes and Views of Three Tree Point* shows the sternwheeler *Multnomah* approaching the dock. Beginning in 1903, this ship was owned by the Olympia-Tacoma Navigation Company. In 1911, she was rammed by the steamer *Iroquois* during a dense fog in Seattle and sank in 240 feet of water. A rancher's possessions were on board and recent dives to the wreck report that the skeletons of the drowned farm animals are still tethered on the deck. (*H. W. McCurdy Marine History of the Pacific Northwest*; dcsfilms.com.)

Another picture from the 1905 real estate brochure shows the sternwheeler *Multnomah* at the dock. On April 1, 1905, the *New York Times* reported that a 50-foot whale came to the surface just ahead of the ship. The whale made a lunge at the ship, frightening the passengers. Captain George Hill rang for full speed astern and ordered preparation for lowering the lifeboats. The whale dove underneath the ship, rubbing its back along the length of her keel. The steamship shook as though she had struck a rock. (The *New York Times*.)

The propeller driven *Arrow* was one of the boats that called at Three Tree Point. The flag on the bow is known as the Jack, and in the United States, it was a blue flag with a star for each state. The *Arrow's* Jack appears to have 45 stars, indicating that it was flown between July 4, 1896, and July 3, 1908. (Puget Sound Maritime Historical Society.)

The sternwheeler *Capital City* was placed on the Seattle-Tacoma-Olympia route in 1900 and was also one of the vessels that stopped at Three Tree Point. In 1902, she collided with a freighter and was holed below the waterline. Capt. Mike Edwards headed for the closest beach near Dash Point and saved the ship and its passengers. (Puget Sound Maritime Historical Society; *Steamers Wake*, Jim Faber.)

The *Flyer* outran nearly every boat on Puget Sound with a cruising speed of 16 knots until the *Tacoma* came along, which had a top speed of 21 knots. Erma Verd, who first came to Three Tree Point in 1905, wrote, "The *Flyer* and *Indianapolis* passed at the point every two hours. We usually went swimming at 4:00 to play in the waves. When I had my canoe, I often went out close to the boats, sometimes between them and took the waves which were huge there! I can remember Mother standing on the porch watching through binoculars. She evidently didn't realize the danger." (Peggy Steele, Puget Sound Maritime Historical Society; *Steamers Wake*, Jim Faber.)

The *Vashon* is seen here leaving the dock at Three Tree Point. The steamer *Burton* was on the same schedule with the *Vashon*, and there were rate wars, races, and collisions as they competed for passengers. On one occasion, the crews of the two boats engaged in a pitched battle using clams as ammunition. The potential cargo of clams ended up in the water or smashed against the side of the steamers. (*H. W. McCurdy Marine History of the Pacific Northwest*; Gordon Peek.)

The *Elwood* was on the Seattle-Olympia run and is one of the boats that called at the dock at Three Tree Point. It had a fairly shallow draft and was able to get very close to the beach. (Puget Sound Maritime Historical Society.)

This 1912 photograph by Asahel Curtis shows, in the foreground, the *Vashon* and the *Crest* next to the dock with the *Flyer* astern of them. They are at the foot of Eleventh Street in Tacoma. The *Vashon* and the *Crest* regularly stopped at Three Tree Point. (University of Washington Libraries, Special Collections, A. Curtis 25095.)

Every day at noon and 3:00 p.m., the *Indianapolis* and the *Tacoma* passed each other off of Three Tree Point. As they passed, they sounded their horns, and local residents used it to tell the time. On December 15, 1930, as they passed each other for the last time, they sounded three long whistle blasts, for it was farewell to the Seattle-Tacoma steamer service. (Puget Sound Maritime Historical Society; *H. W. McCurdy Marine History of the Pacific Northwest.*)

The *Vashon* is just leaving the dock at Three Tree Point, and this view of the stern shows how narrow these boats were. (Gordon Peek.)

In 1928, this tug is hard aground right on the tip of Three Tree Point. Vessels on the beach were always an attraction for local residents. One of the children is using the line over the port side for a swing. (Highline Historical Society.)

The 323-foot SS *Mogul* ran aground on the north side of Three Tree Point on July 17, 1928, at 12:30 a.m. under a heavy pall of smoke from the Quinault forest fire. The ship was bound from Anyox, British Columbia, to Tacoma with a load of copper ore. Two tugs were sent from Seattle to assist in refloating the *Mogul*. The *Equator* towed a scow to the scene to off-load the cargo in the forward part of the ship. (*The Seattle Daily Times*; Highline Historical Society.)

Bright orange ships such as the *Belana* (above) became a familiar sight as they moved freight between Seattle and Tacoma. On this trip, she is carrying some automobiles including a 1941 Plymouth Business Coupe. The opening at the side of the ship contained an elevator used for loading and unloading cargo at any tide. The *Seatac* (below) was built in 1926 and, like most of the fleet, was converted to a towed barge in 1959. (Both Puget Sound Maritime Historical Society.)

Flat rafts or flat log booms were frequently towed past Three Tree Point. If they were bound for Tacoma, they always went between Vashon Island and Three Tree Point because the current in Colvos Passage on the west side of Vashon always flows north. Logs would frequently slip out from under the rafts during towing and then wash up on the beach. (Michael Skalley, Foss Maritime.)

Pictured here in 1936, these men are building a bulkhead using logs that escaped from a passing flat raft. They are, from left to right, Cecil Harper, Guy C. Harper, and Andrew Gray. This bulkhead was so well constructed that it is still in place today. This strenuous work was usually done by the homeowners with help from neighbors and friends. To assist with this task, every family owned at least one pee-vee, which was necessary for moving logs up and down the beach. (Greg Rehmke.)

In this photograph taken in 1961, Douglas Moreland (age 13) is on the beach assisting Cecil Harper (age 67) as he hauls the logs up onto the bulkhead using cable and a hand-crank winch that has been attached to a tree. Douglas was paid 50¢ an hour for this dangerous work.

This bulkhead-building job is heavy-duty work for an older man and a teenaged boy. Cecil Harper and Douglas Moreland are just beginning to move the logs into place in this photograph. (Greg Rehmke.)

Gilbert Duffy recalled a pool party near the beach in 1937. The pilot saw the party and taxied to the cruiser to speak to people on board. The O3U-3 biplane then took off, made a circle, and coming in too low, caught a wing and flipped. The pilot, Bruce Harwood, leaped from the plane and was rescued by Lawrence Feetham (age 15) and Thomas Denovan (age 13), who were boating nearby. Feetham dove in and pulled Seaman William Meyers (age 23) from the rear cockpit. Meyers died soon after being brought to shore. The photograph below shows the navy longboats used to investigate the accident. The plane was from the battleship USS *Arizona*, which was in Bremerton for annual repairs. The *Arizona*'s final resting place is in Pearl Harbor. (Both Gilbert Duffy; Naval Undersea Museum, Navy Region Northwest.)

The fishing trawler *Sea Lion* came ashore on Crescent Beach in the winter of 1949 at the southeast end of Three Tree Point. The boathouse on shore belonged to Birt Fisher. (Museum of History and Industry.)

The purse seiner *Arline* is setting a net on the north side of Three Tree Point, a common sight in the late summer. Residents along the beach could always row out and get a salmon for dinner from the fishermen. (Florence Smallwood.)

In December 1949, a resident of the south beach received a knock on his door in the middle of the night. It was Odd John Solnordal and his engineer Kenneth Ness asking for help after rowing to shore. Their vessel, the *Cape Douglas*, had hit a sharp object, according to Odd John, and sunk in 660 feet of water. The next day, Odd John made an insurance claim on the 78-foot fishing vessel. Several months passed before the insurance company hired a crew to recover the vessel. Using state-of-the-art technology, they miraculously recovered the *Cape Douglas* and found that there was no damage to its hull. Instead, investigators found that all the seacocks had been opened. Odd John was charged with barratry, a maritime law term for willful destruction of a vessel. At his trial, several of his crew testified that Odd John had offered them thousands of dollars to sink the vessel for him. When they refused, he sunk it himself. Odd John was convicted and spent two years at McNeil Island before being deported to his native Norway. (Both Museum of History and Industry.)

In July 1963, Boeing was conducting an acceptance trial of the hydrofoil *FRESH-1*. Col. Vernon Salisbury, a Boeing test pilot, was at the controls, assisted by Peter Sias and Robert Hubbard. Near Three Tree Point, they were traveling at 80 knots and "flying a little high." In an attempt to correct this situation, the nose was pushed down, causing the hydrofoil to yaw and then roll, eventually rolling completely over. It hit the water upside down at 70 knots. The three crew members extricated themselves from the wreck and were picked up by chase boats and taken to shore. A General Construction crane recovered the boat. Even though this hydrofoil set a world record of 96 knots, the navy shifted their efforts to slower vessels and the *FRESH-1* was mothballed. In 1982, the vessel was auctioned and today it is on dry land. Restoration efforts may be underway in the future. (Above, © The Boeing Company; below, Guy Harper; William Ellsworth.)

The USS *South Bend* is shown (above) carrying troops home from World War I in 1919. After the war, the ship was renamed the *J. L. Luckenbach*. On April 26, 1934, the *J. L. Luckenbach* went aground in a dense fog on the north side of Three Tree Point. A picture from the *Seattle Daily Times* (left) shows Highline High School students looking at the ship on the shore. Norton Smallwood (age 19) and his brother, David (age 17), had a leaky rowboat, which they used to ferry the insurance men aboard. The boys climbed aboard the ship, and when it was finally pulled off the beach by the tugs *Goliah* and *Creole*, David was still on the ship. He returned safely the next day. Peggy Steele recalled that her father took her out of school to see the freighter on the beach. She and her sister also rowed around the ship to get a closer look. (Above, Naval Historical Foundation, information from the *Marine Digest*; at left, *Seattle Daily Times*.)

Three

POINTS OF INTEREST

Three Tree Point is a beautiful place to live. As one drives down the hill from Seahurst, he or she can feel the change in the air and breathe a sigh of relief to have arrived home. There are tall fir trees throughout the community, beautiful gardens, interesting homes, and a few landmarks that have been there for generations. There are views of the water, the Olympic Mountains, Mount Rainier, the islands across Puget Sound, and ferries crossing. There is the fragrance of the saltwater and low tide and the invigorating wind off the water. The smell of beach wood burning in a bonfire or fireplace evokes memories. Even the rain and fog come as a welcome sign that another summer is over and a cozy winter awaits.

When the roads were paved between 1920 and 1930, people could come and go in their cars, and many homes were built about that time. Later there was bus service that allowed working people to get to their jobs in Seattle.

As a person travels down Maplewild Avenue, there is a large home on the left that was once the Three Tree Point Clubhouse. Drive a little farther and one will come to the store that has been there for more than a century. Both of these buildings are now private residences, though at one time they were the centers of activity in the community. On a wooded hillside there is a cabin that was built by the Boy Scouts 60 years ago and is still used as a meeting place. Some of the landmark structures are gone, like Gunther's Tower and the water tank above Maplewild Avenue.

Of the three trees that are the symbol of the community, some claim that there is one still standing. Others have said that the last one blew down in the Columbus Day storm of 1962. The navigation light is still on the point, as it has been as long as anyone can remember.

Residents of this peaceful community have always been protective of its traditions and proud of its character and landmarks.

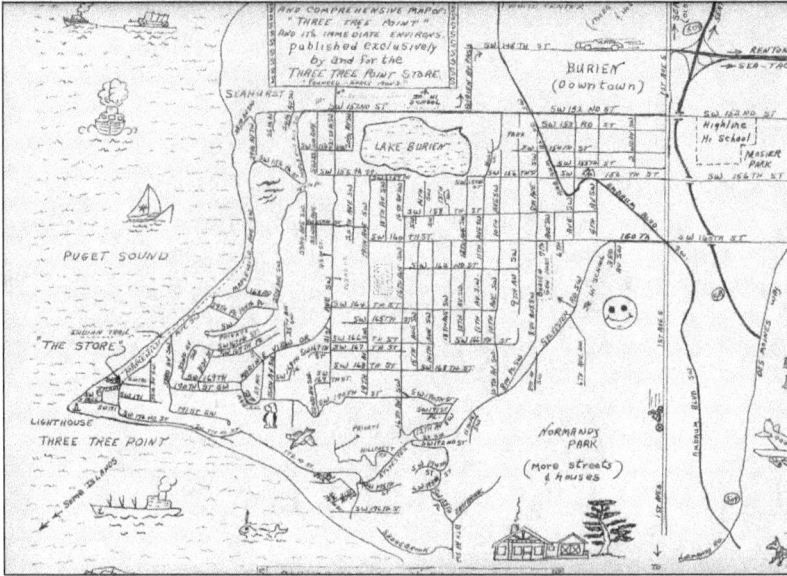

This map was hand drawn by Vi Sparks who was, at one time, the owner of the Three Tree Point Store. This is not drawn to scale but is a fair representation of the street locations in the community. (Ann and Fred Feiertag.)

There have been four bulkheads protecting Three Tree Point. The first was only two feet high, and the land on the property was much lower. During storms, the saltwater flooded the property. Next came a log bulkhead, which was higher, but eventually parts of it were washed away. It was replaced by a cement bulkhead (under construction in this photograph), which was also destroyed by storms; in 1986, it had to be reinforced with a large rock bulkhead. (*Seattle Post-Intelligencer* collection; Museum of History and Industry; Lonnie Miller.)

This aerial shot of Three Tree Point was taken in the 1940s and is facing north toward Arbor Heights. (Lonnie Miller.)

This aerial photograph was taken from directly above Three Tree Point in the 1960s. (Highline Historical Society.)

There were two barges and a tugboat required for building the new rock bulkhead around the point. One barge held a crane and the other held the large rocks that were used. The rock wall was put in front of the old cement wall in 1986. (Both Ray Rice and Andy Ryan.)

An aerial view of the tip of Three Tree Point taken in 1988 shows the large rock bulkhead that was installed in 1986 after years of erosion and multiple attempts to hold back the ravages of tide, wind, and weather from winter in the Northwest. (Lonnie Miller.)

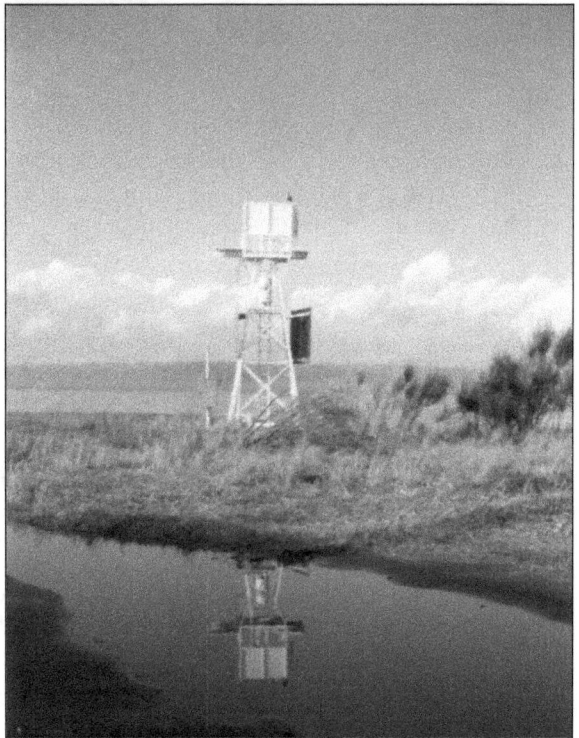

Three Tree Point is a navigational hazard in that the shallow cape intrudes into Puget Sound's deep waters. There was never a lighthouse on Three Tree Point, but there is a minor flashing, five-second navigation light and foghorn. There is also a Vessel Traffic Service navigation light about a mile west of the point. Commercial vessels going north are required to pass between that buoy and the point itself; this often brings the ships quite close to shore. (Lonnie Miller.)

A major access road to the point is 172nd Street, which was paved in sections. This photograph was taken around 1920 just after this section of the street had been paved. Virginia Pearce, who lived on this street in the same house for 89 years, identified the woman walking down the road as Mrs. B. Dinius. "Doc" Sutherland lived on property at the top of the picture. He had a house on one side and a lot across the street where he raised pigs. (Virginia Pearce.)

Sylvester Road is the main arterial leading east of Three Tree Point. At one point, it crosses a deep gully. This photograph was taken in 1935 when a steel and cement bridge was being built to replace the old wooden trestle bridge. The workmen are leaning over the bridge attempting to hoist a wooden beam that is apparently caught underneath it. This concrete bridge is still in place. (National Archives and Records Administration Pacific-Alaska Region.)

This 1936 schedule shows the frequency of the Suburban Transportation System's bus service at Three Tree Point. In those days, a person didn't need a car to travel between Three Tree Point and Seahurst, Burien, or Seattle, as there was service throughout the day.

The girl is standing in front of a 1927 Packard, which dates this picture to about that time. The location is the public access at Maplewild Avenue and 172nd Street Southwest. The house in the background was built in 1919. (Kathy and Todd Anderson; Walter Blair.)

The Three Tree Point Store opened in 1903, and only in recent years has it become a private residence. The car parked in front is a 1930 Desoto. Howard (Howie) Mansfield was an early owner of the store. At the time of this picture in 1937, the building was owned by Myrtle Hutcheson and Gertrude Shields. Subsequent owners were Douglas H. Granberg in 1958, Clara Granberg in 1972, and William Sparks in 1972. Tony McCaffrey was the last person to operate it as a store. The assessor notes that there was an "old service station now used for storeroom." At one time there was a dive shop on the lower level. The building looks much the same today as it did when it was built over 100 years ago. (Walter Blair.)

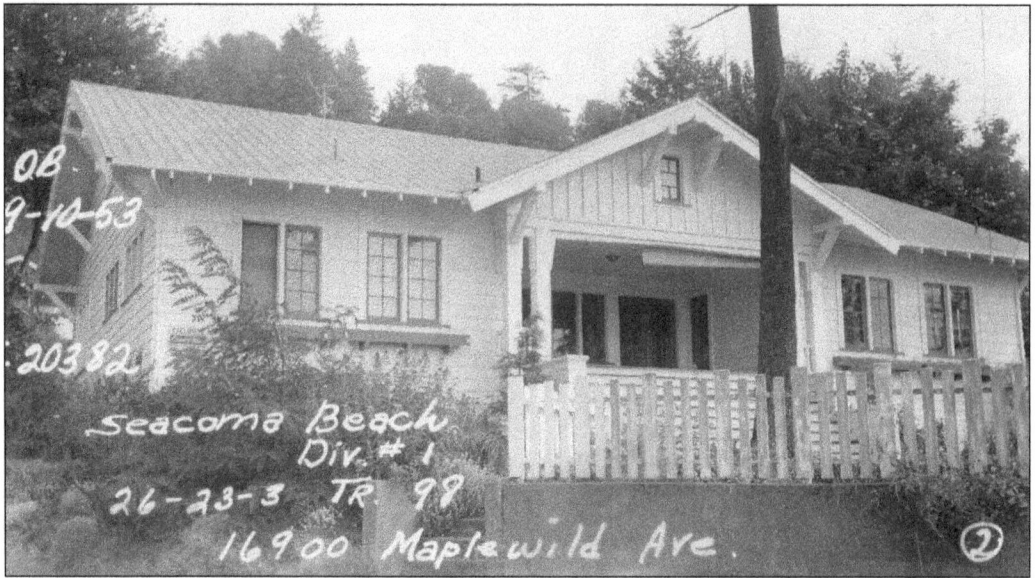

The Three Tree Point Clubhouse was built in 1916 at the corner of Maplewild Avenue and Thirty-fifth Street Southwest. The assessor reports that originally it had 2,280 square feet—all in one room. In front of the building was a clay tennis court with metal strips for lines. This building was used as a community clubhouse until the 1940s, when it became a private residence.

These friends are gathered in 1948 on the porch of the Three Tree Point Clubhouse, which was by then the residence of the Radinsky family. They are, from left to right, (first row) Dick Kraft, Norton Smallwood, Pat Barrett, Diane Radinsky, Pam Smallwood, Sue Kraft, Nancy Smallwood, and Cathy Barrett; (second row) David Smallwood, Mary Smallwood, Bob Siefert, Irv Kraft, Lillian Radinsky, Muriel Siefert, Jean Barrett, Dorothy Kraft, Florence Smallwood, and Joan Kraft; the little girl on the far right is Joanne Radinsky. The parents and children in these families have remained close friends to this day. (Sue Kraft.)

Charles Johnson believes that this is the last remaining tree of the three. It still stands next to the garage of what was the Johnson's family home. Morey Skaret, a 96-year-old retired tugboat captain, began towing on Puget Sound in 1932. He recalled that skippers sounded their horn and counted the seconds it took for the echo to return. Because Three Tree Point was flat, this method wouldn't work. However, on a foggy day the tops of the three trees determined their position.

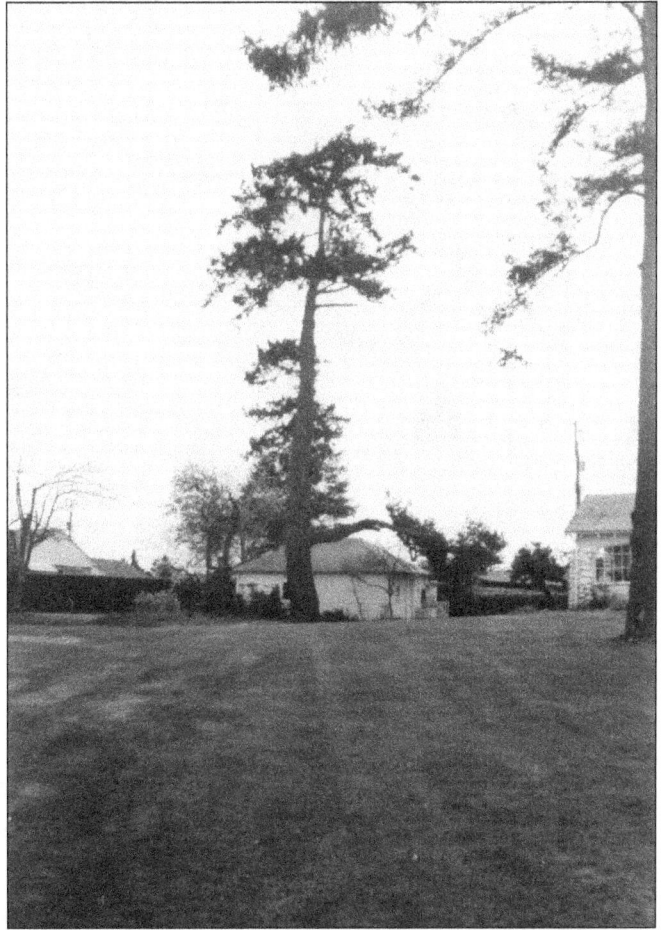

Water District 4 managed this water tank for the community. It was built in 1922, and this picture was taken in 1938. The tank was described as being 18 feet high with a 64-foot circumference and a tar-paper roof. It was located above Maplewild Avenue and may have been fed by the springs that are on that hillside.

55

Located approximately at 152nd Street Southwest and Twenty-second Avenue Southwest in Seahurst, Gunther's Tower was created by a real estate company so that potential property buyers could pick out their lots. This postcard shows a spiral staircase around a large fir tree.

James Wehn created this plaque for his neighbors that reads, "Captian [sic] George Vancouver entered Puget Sound in 1792 naming it after Lieutenant Peter Puget, mountain to the southeast after Rear Admiral Rainier, island to the west after Admiral Vashon. Discovered here in 1936 by Mr. and Mrs. Birt Fisher, the remains of one of the Indians that acted as guide under Chief Kitsap during Vancouvers [sic] surveys." (Davis family.)

In 1949, Boy Scouts of America Troop 377 dedicated their new scout lodge, which was built by their own hands. Special recognition was given to W. E. "Army" Armstrong (kneeling on the right with the service hat on) who was for many years the Scoutmaster of Troop 377. Hundreds turned out to witness the dedication. The Three Tree Point Community Club donated the land on Maplewild Terraces. Arden Steinhart provided the architectural plans, and the Pankrantz Lumber Company donated the lumber. Harold Duncanson bulldozed the ground to get the project started. The lodge is still used today for scout meetings and for other community gatherings. The Three Tree Point Garden Club still sponsors Troop 377 as they did in 1949. (*Highline Times.*)

These two photographs show the range of climate and weather between seasons. The one above shows residents enjoying a record -4.1 tide on a warm June day, looking for lost items and walking where they had never walked before. The tide was out so far that the old pilings from a Mosquito boat dock were exposed. This dock was north of Three Tree Point, near today's Eagle Landing Park in Burien. And in contrast, below is a scene from the south beach after a fierce snowstorm visited the point. (Above, Greg Rehmke; below, Ethan Janson.)

Four

SHACKS AND MANSIONS

Prior to 1936, the King County Assessor records were compiled in longhand on 4-inch-by-6-inch cards with many revisions and cross-outs and no photographs. At that time, many properties were not taxed, and many others were grossly undervalued. In 1936, King County began the King County Land Use Survey, which was financed by the federal Works Progress Administration (WPA). Several hundred Washingtonians were employed to gather data on buildings and property.

As part of the data collected, photographs were taken of nearly every structure in King County. Unless otherwise noted, the photographs in this chapter were taken in 1937 and 1938 and were provided by the Puget Sound Regional Archives. After tabulating data, structures were assigned one of the following values: Class 1—shack; Class 2—modest cottage, slightly superior to shack; Class 3—modest cottage with concrete foundations, built-ins, etc.; Class 4—semi-modern bungalow; Class 5—contract-built modern bungalow, tile floor in bath, hardwood floors; Class 6—architect-built modern residence, frame construction; Class 7—mansion.

King County residents still benefit from this early "stimulus" project, which provided the foundation for the modern property tax system. The ability to revisit every street and country road in the county as it appeared in the late 1930s gives a remarkable perspective on the community's history, one enjoyed by very few others in the country.

Most of the homes in this chapter were built between 1905 and 1925 and included everything from shacks to mansions. Prior to World War II and before the roads were improved, most homes were summer residences. The community of Three Tree Point was almost entirely built out early on, although there have been a few homes constructed in recent years.

Not long after 1923, this picture was taken of Three Tree Point from the upper part of 171st Street. It appears that there are still two of the three trees standing near the point. Several smaller homes have been built on the hillside and some larger, more substantial homes have been constructed along the waterfront. (Highline Historical Society.)

These two cabins were pictured in *Scenes and Views at Three Tree Point*, an early real estate brochure. They were identified as being the summer residences of Samuel Inch and W. W. Noyes, and the cost was from $200 to $350. The exact location of these cottages is unknown, but they appear to be on the north side of the point.

In 1906, Florence and Gilbert Duffy Sr. purchased 42 acres of land north of Three Tree Point. In 1919, they built this home, which was a summer place until about 1930 when it became a year-round residence. Walter Blair has identified the car as a 1926 Star. (Gilbert Duffy.)

This scene is the Duffy's swimming pool looking south toward Three Tree Point. It was built in 1931 and was a saltwater pool. For a while there were only two saltwater pools in the area, Colman Pool in West Seattle and the Duffy pool. Now it is freshwater and home to a koi fish collection. (Wende Duffy.)

This one-room sleeping lodge was built on the Florence Duffy property in 1935. It is constructed of logs and is octagonal in shape. The picture was taken in 1937, and the building was rated by the assessors as "double good." Ten years later, additional rooms were added to the lodge to accommodate the growing family of Gilbert and Eugenia Duffy. (Gilbert Duffy.)

This photograph shows the interior of the one-room log cabin with Gilbert Duffy standing by the fireplace. In an interview just before he passed away in 2009, Gil Duffy said of the cabin, "The trees were from the property. I tried to build it myself, but it was more than I thought. A draw knife will cut through shins same as a log." (Wende Duffy.)

The centerpiece of the Duffy gardens was this lovely bronze statue by artist Dudley Pratt (1897–1975); Duffy claimed that Pratt's wife was the model. Many other important works by Pratt can be seen throughout the Seattle area. The piece is signed and dated 1930. (Wende Duffy.)

This view from above the Pratt sculpture shows how it was placed in the garden. Florence Duffy named her gardens Kewn Gardens, meaning a peaceful place in the forest. She wanted to copy Kew Gardens in England but was advised that the climate at Three Tree Point was not suitable. (Wende and Gilbert Duffy.)

This home was accessed by a long, steep trail from Maplewild Avenue. In 1956, the house sold for $1,500, and in 1962 it was purchased for $19,000. There have been several subsequent owners, but the house has remained basically the same. It recently sold for $693,550. In 1938, the assessor ranked this house as "double very cheap" as far as construction quality, and it was estimated to have a future lifespan of 10 years.

Roy and Hazel Puckett built their lovely new home in 1934, which is when this picture was taken. The Pucketts had four children: Lark, David, Lance, and Melody. The home is still occupied by members of the Puckett family. Previously there was another house on the property, and the log bulkhead was already there supporting that older home. (Lance Puckett.)

Between 1934 and 1937, the old log bulkhead at the Puckett home was replaced with a cement bulkhead. A barge loaded with sand and gravel was beached in front of the house. The cement, stacked in bags, was mixed with the sand and gravel on the barge and then wheeled up to the bulkhead location. The truck had a power take-off on the front end, which ran the cement mixer. (Lance Puckett.)

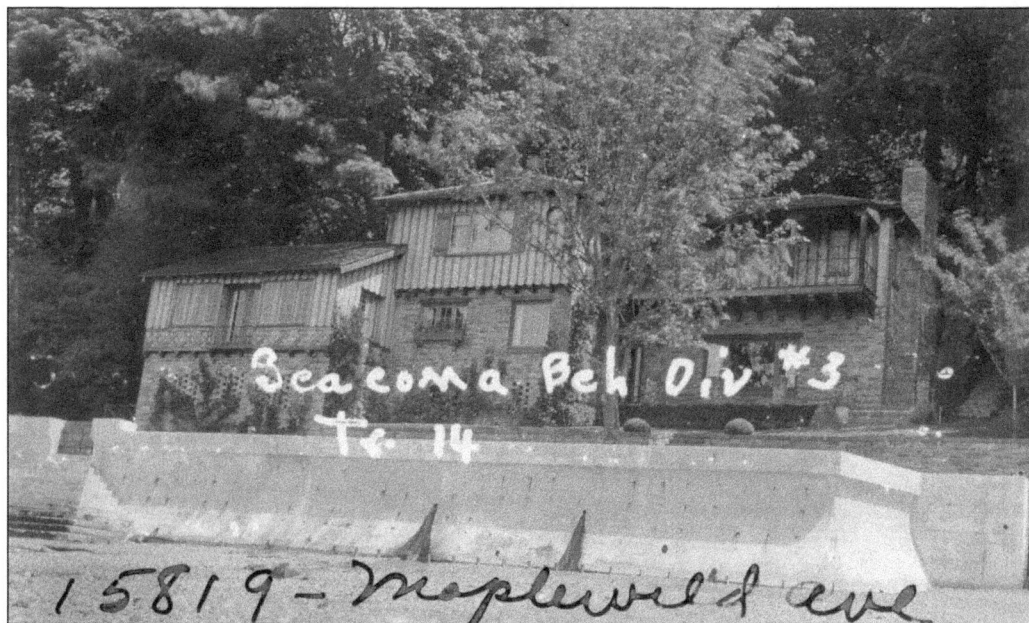

By 1937 or 1938, when the assessors took this picture, the Pucketts had completed the cement bulkhead. This white-painted bulkhead is still in place and is a prominent landmark when looking across the cove on the north side of the point.

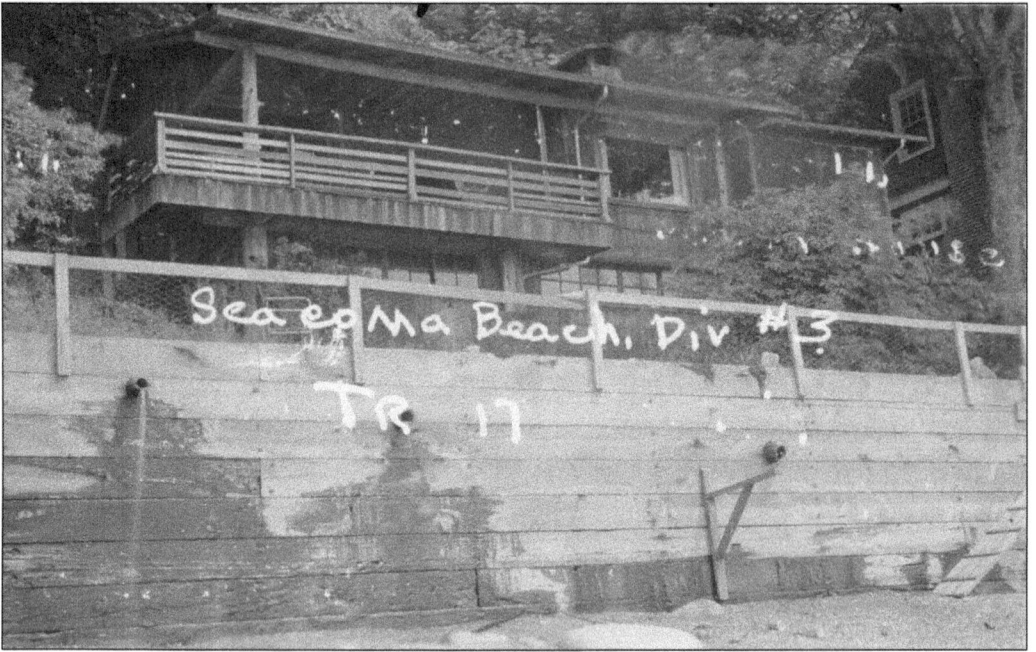

Marie Sayer purchased this property on the north beach in 1915, and the house was built in 1932. In 1957, the property was purchased for $7,400, and a new home was built in the same location. This property has a steep switchback trail going up to Maplewild Avenue, but it has a fabulous view looking across the water towards Three Tree Point, Vashon Island, and the Olympic Mountains. This is one of the locations where springs continuously drain under the property and into the saltwater.

Bill Rehmke is shown here overseeing the construction of one of the many elevators he built over the years to allow Three Tree Point residents to access homes at the base of steep hillsides. (Jonete Rehmke.)

This 1918 home is on the north beach next to the street end and public beach access. In 1927, it was purchased by Leonie Loacker. By 1939, this property was assessed at $1,020, and the records show that it had a future life of 20 years. Ceiling heights were 10 feet in the basement and 10 feet on the main floor.

This house was built in 1918 of "double good" construction and would have been rated as a "mansion" by the assessors. The house sits above Maplewild Avenue with a large lawn sweeping down to street level. A tennis court was constructed behind the house. In 1935, the home was purchased by Harry Gowman, who owned the large Gowman Hotel at Second and Stewart Streets in Seattle, later known as the Stewart Hotel.

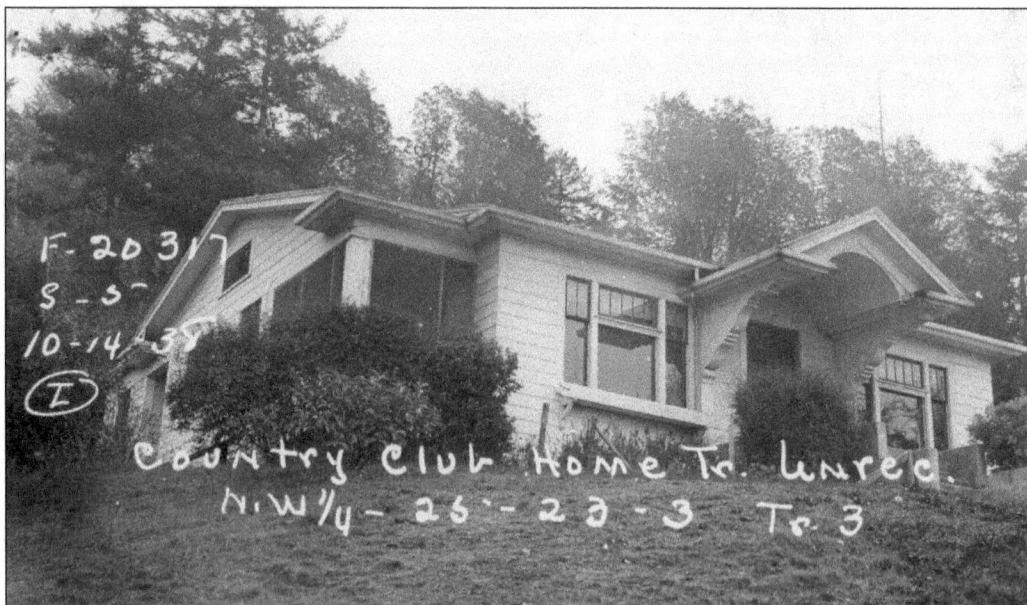

Norton Smallwood, the grandfather of Pam Harper, built this house in 1924. Doug Shadel and his family now live in the house. The construction of the home is very strong, and a story about the home reveals that one of the original trees from Three Tree Point was used to build the house.

In 1916, this large home was built at Crescent Beach at the east end of Three Tree Point. One of the founders of KOMO Radio, Birt Fisher, bought the home in 1935, and the Arnston family purchased it in 1956 for $17,000. It sits on a very large sloping property. Originally there was no kitchen in the main house. The kitchen was in a building near the road due to the fear of fire. There is still a warming oven just outside the door where food was brought down and kept warm for the family. (Lynn and Ralph Davis.)

John Bushell was the first owner of this home located on the south beach. His great-granddaughter still lives in a house along that street. The man on the lowest step is William Bushell; the second man is John Bushell; above John is Andy Bushell, holding Patsy who was born in 1920; the woman above Andy is Adelaide Bushell. (Margaret Boyle.)

This 1920 home is below Maplewild Avenue, and the property crossed the Indian Trail for beach access. The front doors of these homes along Maplewild Avenue were on the waterside of the house, and the back doors traditionally faced the street. Lt. Col. Ray Burgess and his family lived in this house for 25 years. He served in World War I and World War II as an artillery commander. (Robert Burgess.)

This 1917 home is on Maplewild Avenue just north of the store. It lies between the road and the trail and has a 10-foot strip of property leading down to the beach. Portus Baxter and his family lived here at one time. Anna Durand purchased this house in 1934, and the Fullerton family lived here for decades. Their business was a gold mine in Alaska, and they were gone most of the spring and summer months.

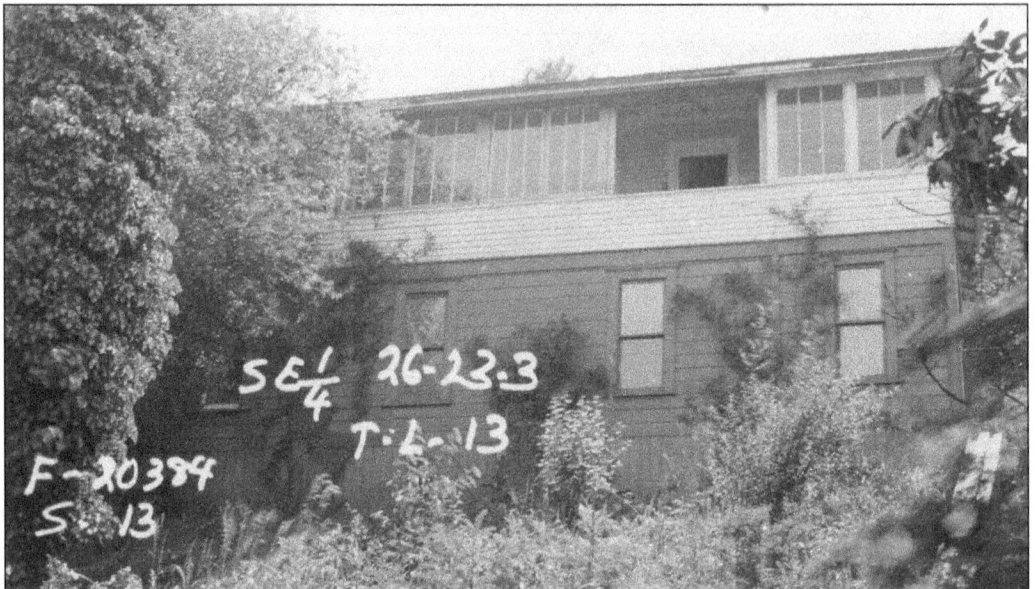

Built in 1905 by Edward T. Verd, this home is one of the first constructed at Three Tree Point. It is on the north side and is accessible from the Indian Trail. The current resident is a granddaughter of the original owners, and the house has been in the family for more than 100 years. Note the hillside track on the right side of the property. Peggy Steele, the current owner, remembers her father building this with a little sled on it that would "zoom" down to the beach or to the water, depending on the tide.

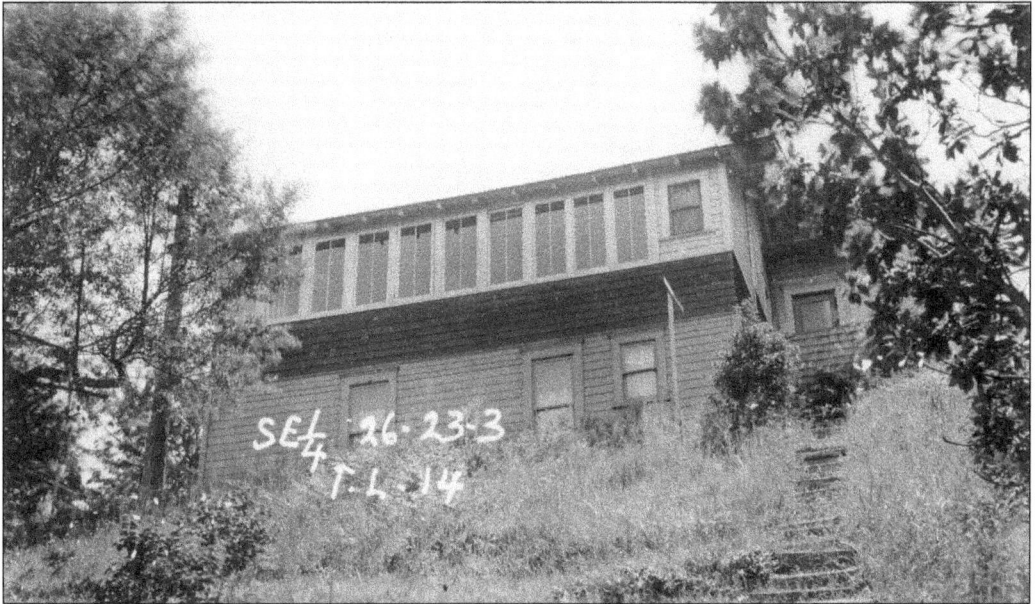

Many homes at the point have been in the same family for several generations. Built in 1905, this home is still owned by the grandson of the original owner and builder. This house and the neighboring house were built by principals in the Bryant Lumber Company of Seattle, and the lumber was brought from Bryant's by boat. This summer home looks much the same today as it did in this 1937 photograph.

This large home is located on the north beach, next to the dock where Mosquito Fleet boats once landed and at the south end of the Indian Trail. It was built in 1913 and remodeled in 1920. L. W. Smith purchased the house in 1926, and Helen and Frank Anderson purchased it in 1952. The current owners bought the house in 1970.

TAX LOT 30
S.E. 1/4 SEC-26-23-3
F-20384
S-30   RES. BLDG. A
6-8-38
(U)

This mansion was located on the north side, not far from the point. The home was built in 1923 by Clark K. Belknap. Mrs. Belknap had at least 100 cats in the house and kept a cow in the yard to provide milk for the cats. One of the last remaining namesake trees is shown in this picture. Subsequent owners were L. D. Brill and Dr. Karl Klopfenstein, who claimed that the big tree fell during the Columbus Day storm in 1962.

TAX LOT 16
S.E. 1/4 SEC-26-23-3
F-20384
S-16   RES. BLDG. A
6-8-38
(U)

This house was on Lot 16, the same property where the navigation light is located. The home was built in 1923 and measured 24 feet by 26 feet. Jean Maguire and her family lived here, and she wrote about their adventures in her book *Beside the Point*, published in 1944. Her book is an amusing and energetic read and mentions several of the neighbors who were there at the time. Later Jim and Glendonna Miller and their children lived in this home.

This view from the water shows 172nd Street and Maplewild Avenue around 1920. The large, dark home on the left was built in 1919 (see next page). Just left of center is the public beach where Maplewild Avenue ends at the water. (Highline Historical Society.)

The same view of the south beach in 2009 shows an unbroken line of homes along 172nd Street. Most of these residents have built beach cabanas on the waterside of the street. (Doug Shadel.)

This home was built in 1919, and in 1936 H. B. and Medina Johnson purchased it. While the Johnsons lived there they kept a pony named Silverbell in the backyard. Robert Brim acquired the house in 1956, and it is still owned by the Brim family. In between those two owners were Bill and Peggy Lindersmith. It is commonly known in the neighborhood as "the Lindersmith house." (Joan Anderson.)

The current residents of this home are an example of families who have remained in the community for generations. They are the grandchildren and great-grandchildren of well-known families who lived at Three Tree Point. Like the older family members, this generation continues to contribute to community activities. This house was built in 1918. When the picture was taken, it was owned by Lucy Corbet.

This large home rests on the bluff above the south beach houses. The property is bisected by the South Indian Trail, which comes up the hill from 172nd Street and Maplewild Avenue and ends at a set of stairs a short distance beyond this home. This house was built in 1920 and has an outstanding view of Puget Sound to the south, Mount Rainier, and the Olympic Mountains.

It is believed that Linden Irwell Gregory (1876–1946) was the original builder of this house, and the neighborhood is now called Gregory Heights. Built in 1929, the construction was rated "double good" by the assessor. In 1939, O. R. Rable purchased the home. This picture was taken in 1964, and the house looks the same today. It sits on the bluff overlooking the south side of the point with a marvelous view of Mount Rainier and Puget Sound to the south.

This home on the south beach was built in 1924. In 1937, it belonged to Florence Custer. John Bausano purchased it in 1964 for $14,000. Note the log bulkhead and the log guardrail still in place in this photograph. Between these homes and the beach is 172nd Street. Their entrances are just steps away from the road.

This home was built in 1919 and was owned by Martha Riggs in 1938. Riggs carried an alarm clock around with her and took the bus whenever she went to town. Laurence Lemmel bought the house in 1959 for $12,000. Note the homes on the hillside above. They were reached by the Moonlight Trail that parallels 172nd Street and runs along the bluff. (Margaret Boyle.)

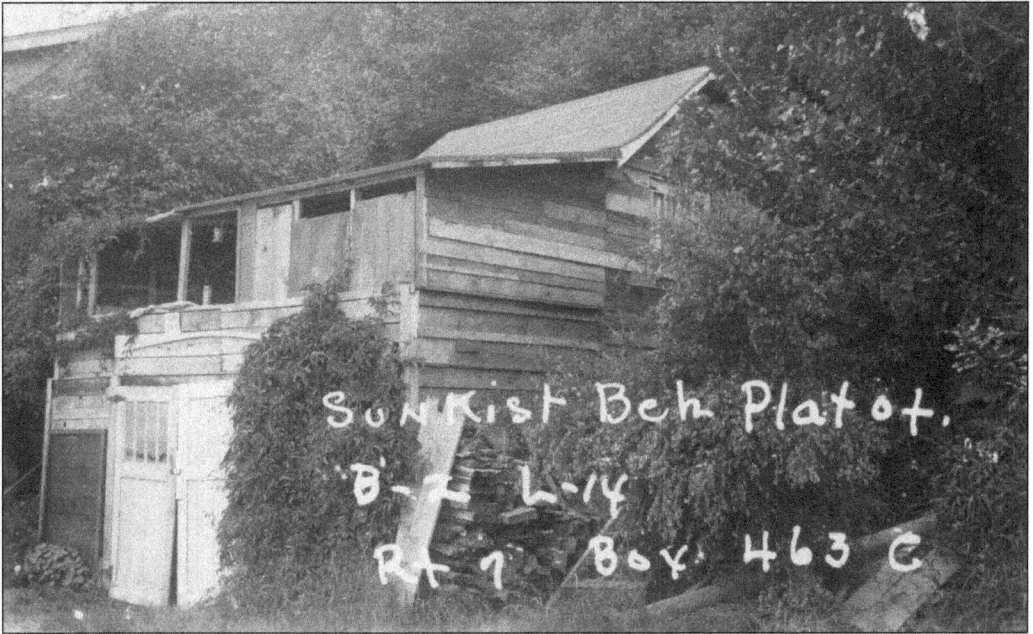

This 1934 home was also owned by Martha Riggs and was categorized by the assessor as a "shack." "The joist on this shack is only driftwood of all sizes. Same with the post," commented the assessor in 1938.

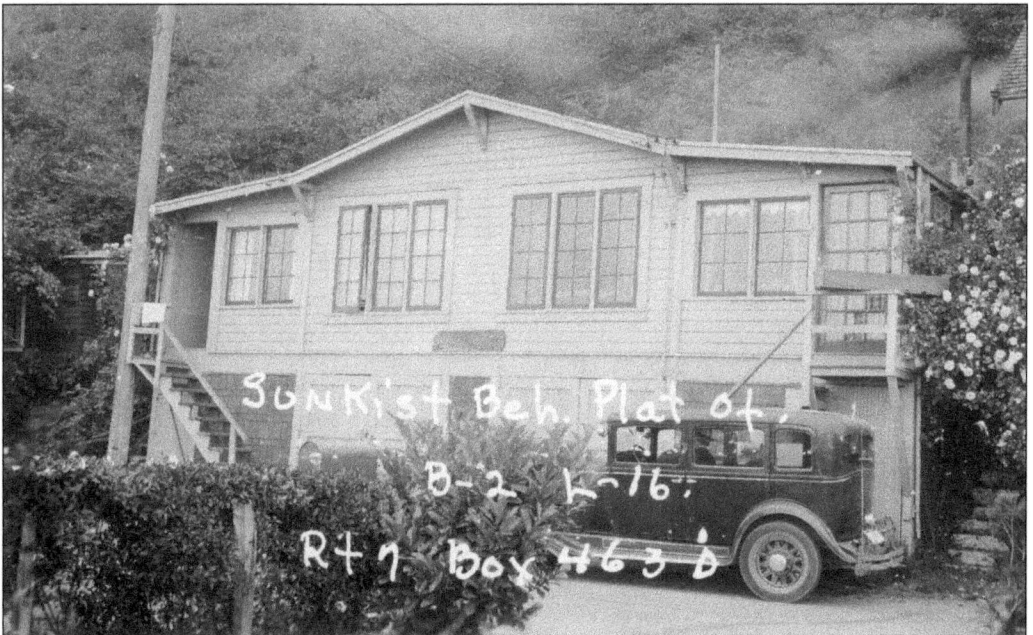

This duplex was built in 1925 and in 1938 was owned by George Jorgenson. The building was converted to a single-family home, and during the 1940s the Zellweger family lived here. The house was paneled in knotty pine, and the room on the left had a built-in bed. Flowers grow profusely with this southern exposure, as seen by the climbing roses on the right. The car dates from about 1930.

F. W. Cox built this south beach home in 1926. It was torn down in 1955 when it was purchased by the Boyles. Andy Bushell gave half of the lot next door to his daughter and son-in-law, and their existing home was built on that site. (Margaret Boyle.)

This home was built in 1920 and purchased in 1922 by Richard G. Bushell. Andy and Adelaide Bushell and their four daughters—Patricia, Mary Jean, Margaret, and Salle—lived here. The house was torn down in 1961. There are now two properties totaling 120 feet where there had originally been three 40-foot lots. (Margaret Boyle.)

While this home has had several owners, it is known locally as the Tritle house. The couple owned Tritle's Glycerin and Rosewater in Burien where they manufactured and sold lotion and other products. The Tritles gave the wild and inaccessible hillside behind their house to the Audubon Society. (Three Tree Point Garden Club.)

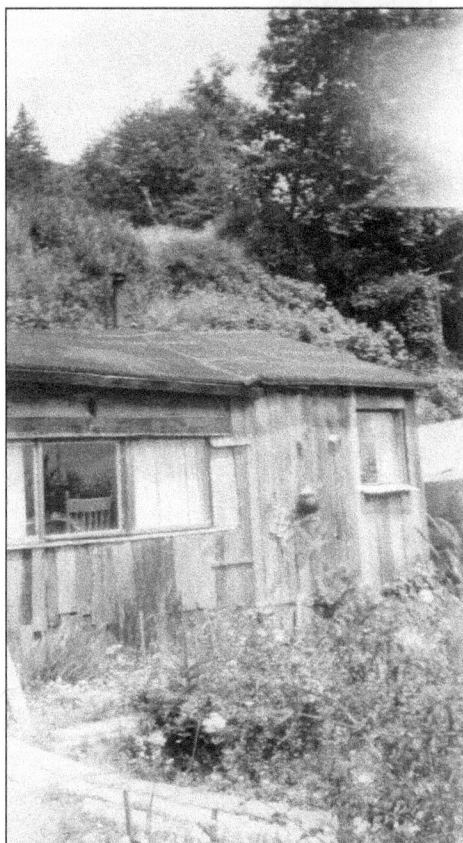

This summer home would have been rated as a "shack" by the assessor's men. It was located at the east end of the south beach below 172nd Street. David J. and Zelma Williams used an outboard boat to move their family and belongings from Dolphin Point on Vashon Island into the cabin in 1936. (David and Mary Williams.)

This *c.* 1928 photograph was taken from the water and shows several homes at the east end of 172nd Street where the road starts up the hill. The very skillfully constructed log bulkhead is being admired by a resident who may be looking for a way down to the beach. Note the sand pits visible on the right. The automobile parked on the bulkhead is a 1925 Dodge. (LaVerne McIntyre and Walter Blair.)

These two men are standing beside their automobile on the east end of the unpaved 172nd Street just before the road goes uphill. A photograph taken today would show a solid row of houses on the upper side of the road and many beach cabanas on the right side. (David Wintermute.)

Five

A PLACE TO PLAY

The Duwamish Tribe used well-established trails to walk to Three Tree Point, a place for which they had several names. In the summer they came to dig clams, gather berries, and meet people from the other villages. There was freshwater in abundance, lovely beaches, and sunshine.

The Three Tree Point Development Company touted it as an ideal place for a vacation or weekend getaway. This has always been a place to play.

Two Indian trails provide excellent views of the sound and delightful hiking in any weather. There are no parks at the point; instead, children have played on the beach or in empty lots and woods. The logs and planks that washed up on the beach were used to build swimming rafts as soon as school was out. Children took off their shoes on the first day of summer and kept them off until school started again. In a few days, their feet were tough enough to run on the rocky beach.

Salmon fishing has traditionally been a very popular sport, and fishing derbies have been an annual event. Most people owned at least one boat, which children became comfortable using.

In the early days, children and adults would swim every day. In the 1950s, waterskiing became popular, and several fortunate teens had speedboats powerful enough to pull one or two skiers. The north side of the point is a well-known scuba diving location, and there was once a dive shop at the Three Tree Point Store.

In the 1920s and 1930s, there was a clubhouse for dances and parties and a clay tennis court for neighbors to use. The Fourth of July has always been a big event with a parade, picnics, and fireworks. In the winter when it snowed, there was a bonfire at the foot of Maplewild Avenue, and children, as well as some brave adults, would go to the top of Gregory Heights and coast down to the bonfire.

Three Tree Point has provided generations with fond memories and will continue to do so well into the future.

The annual Three Tree Point Fishing Derby was started in 1937, when a group of men calling themselves the Beachcombers Betterment Association met in Herb Johnson's basement. All types of boats were used in the early fishing derbies. The large cruiser is a Lake Union Dreamboat. The small cruiser near shore is a Mukilteo design and on the lower right is a 14-foot Reinell. (Chuck Johnson; Kathy and Todd Anderson.)

After a derby in the 1940s, the participants line up for a photograph. Pictured from left to right, standing in the second row starting in the center, are Andy Bushell (white shirt), Burt Gustafson, Julius Radinsky (suit coat), unidentified, David Smallwood, Bill Palmer, unidentified, Irving Kraft, two unidentified, and Norton Smallwood; kneeling in front in the white pants is Bill Lindersmith. (Charles Johnson and Joan Anderson.)

The men and boys are gathered waiting for the fishing derby prizes to be awarded. This took place on the property at the corner of 172nd Street and Maplewild Avenue. The boy kneeling on the left is Charles Johnson and behind him is Bill Palmer; Norton Smallwood is the man on the right with the pipe. This picture was taken in the 1940s. (Charles Johnson.)

In the 1940s, Ken and Ann Hadfield hosted the breakfast after the derby. The man in the plaid shirt is Phil Yarno; the man on the far right is Eric Sander; in the center is Julius Radinsky; to the right of Radinsky is Irv Kraft (smiling). The men always teased Julius because he wore a suit and tie to the derby. (Kathy and Todd Anderson; Diane Radinsky Wall.)

Bob Boaz was the master of ceremonies at the fishing derbies. Here he is showing off some of the prizes—fishing poles and a nice wooden tackle box. Eric Sander is the gentleman in the hat in the foreground. (Kathy and Todd Anderson.)

At this fishing derby in 1954, these men must have caught the prize-winning fish. They are, from left to right, Bob Manola, Bill Boyle, Floyd Fleming, and Joe Manola. Joe's granddaughter now organizes the fishing derbies at the point. (Kathy and Todd Anderson.)

It looks like the women are serving up the food after the derby while the boys are climbing all over the 1939 or 1940 International truck. The women in the foreground are, from left to right, Babe Manola, unidentified, Ann Byers, and Elsie Fleming. (Kathy and Todd Anderson.)

Back in 1938, fish were plentiful and large as these king salmon attest. Eric Sander (called Fafa by his family), his granddaughter Svea, and his son Art Sander are posing with their catch. Svea does not appear too happy about having to hold these newly caught fish. (Sandra Sander Noreen.)

Bob Manola sits in his boat waiting for the derby to start. Bob and his brother Joe had a barbershop in Burien and lived at Three Tree Point. (Kathy and Todd Anderson.)

Larry Searle (left) and Eric Sander are helping Goldie "Mimi" Sander into the boat while a young Julie Sander looks on. The motor is a 1947 five-horsepower Johnson. The Searle and Sander families lived at Crescent Beach, east of Three Tree Point. The picture was taken about 1947. (Sandra Sander Noreen.)

In the 1930s, swimming in Puget Sound was a daily summertime event. These three children did not even stop to put on their suits. The water was too inviting, and the rowboat was drifting away. In Puget Sound, the water temperature varies little through the year. In the summer it averages about 55 degrees Fahrenheit. It may be warmer at this location because it is relatively shallow. It was customary to wait until the tide came in over the hot sand. (Greg Rehmke.)

The cold water didn't stop the Guthrie children—from left to right, Joan, Frank, and Nancy—from enjoying a swim on the north beach about 1935. Joan and Frank still live in Seahurst, the community just to the north of Three Tree Point. (Greg Rehmke.)

In 1928 or 1929, local residents celebrate this birthday on the south beach. In the back row on the left is Margaret Bushell and on the right is Adelaide Bushell; in the middle row on the right is Lydia Bushell Ramsay; the others are unidentified. The dark brown house is the Priestly home. The Dunbar family lived next door in the tent on the beach. (Margaret Boyle.)

This was the Independence Day children's parade of 1928. Leading the parade is George Priestly and next to him is his sister Cecily. George and Cecily were fortunate in that their father was a salesman for the Hitt Fireworks Company. Every August he would gather large quantities of unsold "big stuff," huge skyrockets and mortar bombs, and put on a show for the neighborhood. (Margaret Boyle and Norton Smallwood.)

Above is a group of children in the 1980s getting ready to start the Fourth of July parade—always a favorite in the Three Tree Point community. Nick Miller is sitting on the hood of the car and his siblings, Baron (left) and Mercedes, are riding behind him; the boy riding the bicycle is Toby Reed. The picture below shows the start of the same parade in 2009. (Above, Lonnie Miller; below, Michael Brunk, www.b-townblog.com.)

Pictured here on the Fourth of July 1989, Lonnie Miller is being crowned Queen of Three Tree Point by Jane Cancro at the flag-raising ceremony. Dr. Lynn Frary played the trumpet for the event. (Lonnie Miller.)

Neighborhood kids assist in a 2009 flag-raising ceremony. They are, from left to right, Brooks Schaeffer, Sophie Schaeffer, Sammie Box, Stella Fosberg, unidentified, Vica Dow, Ryan Pederson, Emily Shadel, Alec Fursman, and Carsten Kleitsch; the adults to the right are Scott Schaeffer and outgoing Three Tree Point King Jerry Robinson (far right); Andy Kleitsch is leading the ceremony. (Michael Brunk, www.b-townblog.com.)

The community raises thousands of dollars each year to fund this spectacular fireworks exhibition. A barge is towed into place at the end of the point, and around 10:00 p.m. the show begins, ending a daylong celebration that includes a pancake breakfast, flag-raising ceremony, children's parade, and dozens of parties. (Michael Brunk, www.b-townblog.com.)

Family and neighbors gather here on the beach to have their picture taken. From left to right they are (first row) Margaret Bushell, Mary Jo O'Brien, and an unidentified young woman; (second row) Salle Bushell, Lillian Nelson and child, Dickie Wilson, Marion Wilson, Adelaide Bushell, and Pat Bushell; (third row) Andrew Bushell. The car in the background is a 1934 Chevrolet. (Margaret Boyle and Walter Blair.)

On a wonderful summer day in 1936, two "Guys" are rowing in a boat. The Guy rowing is Guy M. Harper, four years old; the Guy in the stern is his uncle Guy C. Harper. Fifteen years later, Guy M. stroked the University of Washington Freshman Crew to a national title. A year later, in 1952, he stroked the UW shell to a third-place finish in the Olympic Trials.

The Smallwood family has gathered here in 1951 for a picture in front of their home on the north beach. From left to right they are (first row) Norton Smallwood Jr. and his Irish setter Bridget; (second row) Rob Smallwood, Nancy Smallwood, and Kathy Smallwood; (third row) Mary Smallwood (Rob and Kathy's mother) and Norton and Florence Smallwood (parents of Norton Jr. and Nancy). Norton Smallwood Sr.'s grandparents lived at Three Tree Point, and now his great-granddaughter lives there, completing six generations of the Smallwood family.

Every generation has built forts, and in 1952 these children chose to build one near the beach. Posing from left to right are Brian Guptil; Bob, Steve, and Kathy Finch; Bonnie Bjornson; and Randi Boyle. The house in the background belonged to Peter Colman. (Margaret Boyle.)

In this photograph, the boy appears to be suspended in air because the diving board is lined up with the horizon. The board was mounted on a raft constructed by the boys. The sailboat in the background is an 18-foot Falcon. In the far distance is the northern tip of Vashon Island. This picture was taken in the early 1950s.

Around 1960, these boys are having a great time using a dock and diving board constructed on the north side of the point. Douglas Downs is the boy with his arms up, and Jim Holden has his arms down. Both of them are about to fall into the water.

This cruiser has anchored so that the boys could dive off and swim around to the swim step—again and again. Children learned to swim and dive in Puget Sound.

As the tide came in, boat owners had to keep pulling up the boats that were on the beach. A particular concern was when freighter waves came in, as they could swamp the boat. Steve Purcell is pulling up his grandfather's *Atsamaboat* around 1967. In the background is a Bell Boy outboard boat belonging to the Burgess family.

Building a raft was a necessity for children who lived along the beach. These boys erected a tent on their raft, hoping to sleep overnight there. However, they found that the raft was frequently awash. They had to abandon that idea and ended up sleeping on the beach instead. The boys are Brad Smallwood (left) and Michael Purcell.

Peggy Steele talked about building a raft every summer, "There were lots of wonderful planks because the big old freighters would come into Elliott Bay, and all the cargo on the deck would be braced with planks which they'd throw overboard and then it'd come floating down here. So we'd get our pee-vee and go cruising up and down the beach and find a good cedar log. Then we'd tow it home with the rowboat or just wade and push it here." The children on this well-built raft are Steven Leech and Michelle Purcell.

Florence Smallwood and her granddaughter Nancy Purcell have been swimming and are taking a lunch break. Florence was a well-known teacher at Lake Burien Elementary School. She loved to swim and would often dare others to go in with her. The brave ones would hold hands and run in all at once. This picture was taken in the early 1970s.

In 1969, KVI Radio personality Robert Hardwick announced an event called the Dinghy and Survival Derby. This boat race started in Ballard, proceeded through the ship canal and locks, and into Shilshole Bay. Several fellows from Three Tree Point entered a raft called "The Lusty Wench" from the nonexistent Three Tree Point "Yaught Club." Dressed in nightgowns from left to right are David Puckett, Guy Harper, Richard Anderson, William Wintermute, and Robert Cole. This fine craft consisted of a bed with life cushions. Their raft won first place—a year's supply of Dag's 17¢ hamburgers and $50, which they used to start the real Three Tree Point Yacht club.

Tom Ables is at the helm of his 17-foot Lyman outboard with a Seattle Yacht Club burgee on the bow. Tom, who lived near the point, was a dentist and always had the latest in boats, including a Chris-Craft cruiser that was used extensively during the summer. He was noted for having wonderful beach bonfires and parties.

One of the most popular sports beginning in the 1950s was waterskiing. In this photograph, two skiers are being pulled behind an outboard in the cove on the north side. Norton Smallwood Jr. reports that in the early 1950s they made their own skis in eighth-grade wood shop, including banana skis for slalom and a pair of shoe skis that were about 18 inches long and had no fins.

The 30-foot *Eleanor* was built in 1929 for L. C. Smith of the Smith typewriter fame. It had a 992-cubic-inch Hall Scott Defender engine. The U.S. government conscripted the boat during World War II, as it reached a speed of over 50 miles per hour. In 1951, W. J. Miller of Three Tree Point bought the boat and named it *Eleanor* after his mother. Norton Smallwood Jr. wrote, "We would hear the distinctive throaty roar of an engine off the point and would know that the *Eleanor* was out prowling the Sound." Below, Stan Lemmel jumps a tugboat's wake in what was a common activity off the point. Traveling in excess of 40 mph, small boats would run head-on into the wakes of ships and tugs and fly completely out of the water. (Above, Lonnie Miller; below, Stan Lemmel; Bud Melby and Norton Smallwood Jr.)

A big wave from a harsh winter storm crashes against the bulkhead of Phil Fleming's cabana as a friend looks on in amazement. The severe weather stripped away a fresh paint job on the building. (Phil Fleming.)

Colleen Scott windsurfs along the waters west of Three Tree Point in 1979. For decades, adventurous residents have challenged weather conditions and shipping-lane traffic to experience the thrill of windsurfing.

The newest rage at Three Tree Point is kite surfing. This intrepid soul challenges the freighter *Spirit* in mid-channel off the point with the crew of a small pleasure craft looking on in disbelief. (Ethan Janson.)

A kite surfer steers onto the beach at Three Tree Point to take a breather after a rigorous workout in a strong October wind. (Doug Shadel.)

Many residents of the point have owned sailboats over the years. *Yankee Devil* was a Spencer 35 owned by Richard Rehmke, standing in the stern. Others aboard are Chris Spaun on the bow, Georgia McClaren lying on the port side, Greg Rehmke near the mast, and in the cockpit Joan Rehmke with Dorie Anderson at the helm; Margaret Rehmke is behind her Dad. (Greg Rehmke.)

In 1971, the Boy Scouts of America and members of the Three Tree Point Yacht Club formed Explorer Post 950 to teach teenage boys and girls how to sail. Donated sailboats were used, and the scouts won many races on Puget Sound. They entered the 41-foot *Heather* in the 1981 Swiftsure Race, the most prestigious yachting event in the Pacific Northwest. The course was 136 miles long, and the race lasted over 34 hours. Fred Roswald was the adviser, and Steven Purcell was the skipper. EP950 and *Heather* won the race on corrected time and are now in sailing history books as the official winner of the 1981 Swiftsure Race. (Pacific Yachting.)

A perfect day is racing a sailboat with a lot of wind and Mount Rainier in all its glory. This is the *Assault* with its crew of high school students, members of Explorer Post 950. This picture was taken in the early 1980s. A series of quality boats were donated to the Boy Scouts and raced by EP950 for many years. Several hundred young people learned to sail as part of this program.

The 6-meter *Lully II* (left) was another boat donated to Explorer Post 950. It was the same Norwegian boat that took a silver medal in the 1936 Olympics in the Bay of Kiel, Germany. Before it was donated, it had been converted to a cruising six and then neglected for many years. The Scouts and their leaders restored the boat to its original racing configuration.

Bill Rehmke was an engineer who designed and built most of the hillside elevators at the point. In 1967, he was sailing alone in Puget Sound when he noticed a squall heading his way. Going forward to secure the jib, he fell overboard without a life jacket and surfaced just in time to see the transom of his boat moving away. Bill waved frantically at a passing freighter. He was rescued and then transferred to a yacht that helped him retrieve his sailboat. He returned to the marina wet, cold, and extremely lucky. (Greg Rehmke.)

Six

CHARACTERS AND
CREATURES OF THE POINT

One of the unusual facts about Three Tree Point is that there are many families who have lived at the point for multiple generations, sometimes in the same house or nearby. One woman lived in her home for 89 years. Others live in homes built by their grandparents over 100 years ago. The point's pure magic is the prime reason families remain or return in later years. Friendships have been made that have lasted for generations, as if they were family members. Neighbors assisted each other with major projects like building bulkheads, home additions, and the maintenance of the clubhouse and scout cabin. During World War II, neighbors took turns climbing a watchtower on the point, looking for enemy planes that might come in low over Puget Sound. They made a party out of this event and looked forward to taking their turn.

The point has been home to the wealthy and the not so wealthy, but money, house size, and status have never seemed to matter in this egalitarian community. The point has always seemed to attract interesting people. There have been businessmen and women, journalists, artists, and entertainers. There have always been fishing derbies, Fourth of July celebrations, parties, picnics, and dances. Organizations like the Three Tree Point Garden Club and the Boy Scouts have been in existence for decades. In the early days, most children went to Lake Burien Elementary School, and the school and churches in Burien and Seahurst were centers of activity for families.

For children it was a marvelous place to grow up. There were the Indian trails for exploring and the sandpits for running and leaping. There were vacant lots for football and wooded lots for building forts. Children grew up feeling comfortable in boats and learned to swim in the cold water. Norton Smallwood Jr. wrote, "My childhood friends and I had no doubt in our minds that the Three Tree Point community was ours to do with what we wished. The resident adults were tolerated only as providers of food and shelter during our down time."

Finally, Three Tree Point has been home to an amazing array of non-humans: bald eagles, osprey, heron, seagulls, kingfishers, hummingbirds, raccoons, foxes, sea lions, and killer whales. Whether it is generation upon generation of human characters or diverse groupings of other creatures, Three Tree Point continues to teem with life.

George and Lula Sylvester came to Seattle from Boston in the early 1880s. They were "very comfortable" and wanted to build a road so they could drive to their property on Three Tree Point. George built Sylvester Road from First Avenue South to his beachfront property around 1910. This photograph, taken in 1914 along 172nd Street, shows George trying to dig his car out of the gravel while Lula waits on the log guardrail. (Gregory Worthing.)

Lula Sylvester (right) and a friend are standing next to the log rail in a different location along the south beach. Lula and George Sylvester had no children and adopted Helen Furness Worthing, treating her like a daughter. Lula was also an artist and a quilter, and her work is still cherished by the heirs of Helen Worthing. (Gregory Worthing.)

These five young people are having a picnic on the beach at Three Tree Point around 1910. Before there were disposable cups, it looks like they used fine china teacups. (Gregory Worthing.)

Roy Puckett and his family lived on the north side of the point. After World War I, brothers Jim and Roy Puckett founded the Puckett Company. Canned salmon was shipped from Alaska to their company in Seattle, where the cans were labeled and then forwarded to grocery outlets throughout the country. They retained ownership of this company, located at Piers 24 and 25, until 1973. (Lance Puckett.)

Norton Smallwood was born in 1915 and appears to be about two years old in this picture. His grandparents had a summer place on the south beach, and his parents built a home on Thirty-fifth Avenue. Norton lived at Three Tree Point all of his life. In the background of this picture is the public dock that was located at Crescent Beach. Some of the piling from this dock is still visible today. (Florence Smallwood.)

This picture of Jack and Donna Hanton was taken about 1920. They were the children of Francis Pontine "Gypsy" and John Hanton. Brother and sister are walking on Maplewild Avenue before the road was paved, which is believed to have been completed about 1931. (Greg Rehmke.)

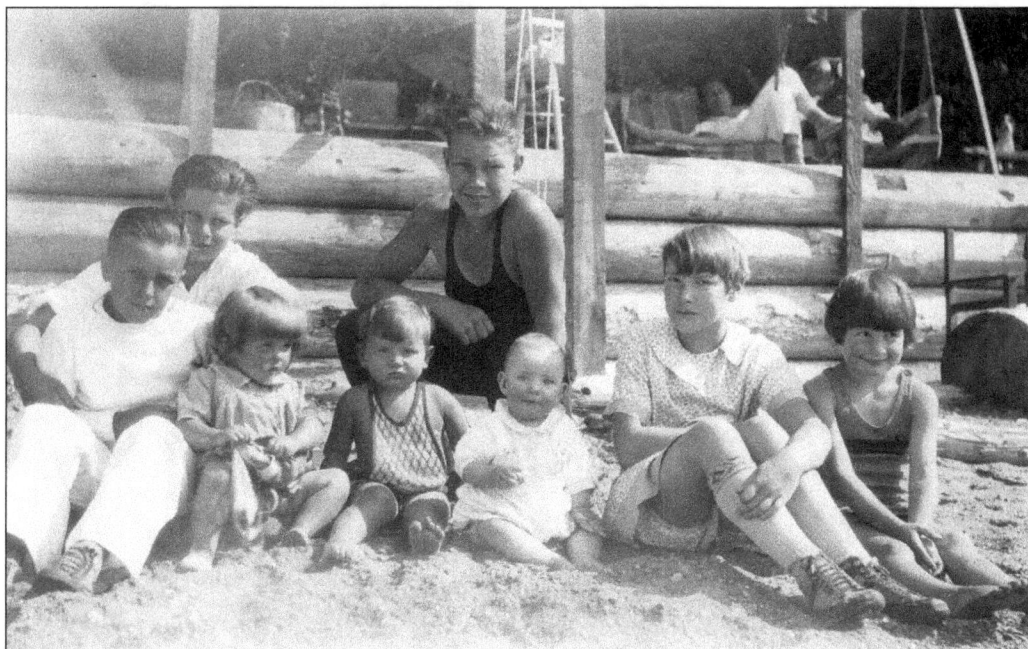

These children are having their picture taken in front of a log bulkhead in 1929. The cousins are, from left to right, (first row) Bob Harper, Letty Harper, Frank Guthrie, Pam Harper (not the author), Donna Hanton, and Nancy Guthrie; (second row) Bill Harper and Jack Hanton. Only one of the children in the picture, Frank, is alive today.

In 1937, the Holderness family had a Halloween party for their daughter and her friends. They are, from left to right, (back row) two unidentified boys, Bill McShane, Bill Holderness, Mary Holderness, and an unidentified girl; (front row) the only child identified is Nona Jansen, second from right. (Sallie Holderness.)

Florence Adelaide Blethen Duffy was the daughter of Col. Alden Duffy, the founder of the *Seattle Times*. Florence and Gilbert L. Duffy Sr. purchased their property north of Three Tree Point in 1906. There was originally 42 acres on the property, and up until 1930 it was only a summer home for the Duffy family. (Gilbert Duffy and Wende Duffy.)

Florence Duffy's son and his family pose on the porch of their home. They are, from left to right, (first row) Eugenia (known as "Cookie"), April, and Wende; (second row) Gilbert Jr., Jinx, and Joanne. By the time Wende came along, they had outgrown their house on the beach, and in 1953 they built a large, new home on the property. The Duffys tied the knot in 1943 and were married for 63 years. (Wende Duffy.)

Gilbert Duffy is shown with his prize-winning 1933 Duesenberg he called "The Duesy." Gil attended car meets and won awards for his car, including many Best in Show ribbons. He donated a number of vintage automobiles to museums, including two vintage fire trucks to the Last Resort Fire Department in Ballard, Washington. (*Highline Times*; Wende Duffy.)

Robert and Ruth Conrad arrived in Seattle in 1939, having moved from Fresno, California. The Three Tree Point Store was for sale, and when they drove down the hill from Seahurst and Mrs. Conrad saw the location and the huge yard with the house so close to the beach she said, "This is like living in a resort area." They bought the store and moved into the attached residence before Christmas with their son and daughter. The store was open seven days a week in the summer. They delivered groceries and gave credit to customers. The Conrads sold the store in the spring of 1951 and then opened stores in Sunnydale and West Seattle. Robert Conrad lived to be 86, and his wife lived to be 94. (Mary Ellen Conrad Gettmann.)

These friends have gathered in a picnic shelter on the south beach in 1945. They are, from left to right, Norton Smallwood, Irving Kraft, Dorothy Kraft, and Bob Boaz in the hammock; the other two women and baby are unidentified. (Susan Kraft.)

Andy Bushell (right) was a well-known figure at Three Tree Point. In this picture, he is shown as a member of the Sheriff's Auxiliary with an unidentified partner. Andy was a member of the family that owned and operated Bushell's Seattle Auction for 98 years. Andy's grandfather John lived at Three Tree Point as did his father, Richard—all on the south beach. The fourth and fifth generations still live on the same property. (Margaret Boyle.)

Lake Burien Elementary was the school that Three Tree Point children attended. It was originally built in 1914, and a new building was put up in 1926 to accommodate the increasing population. Students from the point walked to school until 1929, when the first school bus was provided. It was a Model T Ford truck with benches and curtains along the sides. Lake Burien was a public school for another 50 years. Freeman J. Mercer (back row, far right) was principal from 1924 to 1952 and taught classes for 17 years. Mercer also lived at Three Tree Point. (Sallie Holderness Tostberg.)

Glendonna Miller is loved by all who know her. She had a lot of troubles in her life yet was always happy and fun loving. Here she is on the beach in front of the bulkhead at the point sometime between 1948 and 1951. The U.S. Coast Guard delivered bulbs for the navigation light, and Glendonna was in charge of making sure that it was operating correctly. For that she was named Seaman 3rd Class. (Lonnie Miller.)

The Miller family is shown here in front of their home in 1951. They are, from left to right, (first row) "Grandma Dudley" holding Beau, Eleanor, and William "Buck" Miller holding Deidre; (second row) Jim and Glendonna Miller. The Millers lived right on the point for 62 years. Buck Miller started a company that manufactures sawmill equipment, which is now run by his great-grandchildren. (Lonnie Miller.)

Nellie Lolita Medina (Dena) Johnson (1903–1983) moved to Three Tree Point with her husband in 1933. Her children, grandchildren, and great-grandchildren still live at the point. Dena loved to swim and would do so all along the south beach. However, in 1945, she was diagnosed with a nervous system disorder, and for the rest of her life she used a golf cart to get around. Nevertheless, Dena hosted fishing derby parties and crab feeds and had many friends among the neighbors. (Charles Johnson.)

Dena Johnson's daughter Joan poses with her husband, Einar, and their children, Susan and Todd, on Easter Sunday on the lawn in front of her parents' home. Sadly, Einar passed away suddenly when Todd was just 15. Joan still lives at her home on the beach, just steps from where she grew up, with her daughter and family next door and her son and family just down the street. (Kathy and Todd Anderson.)

Joe and Jeannette "Babe" Manola moved to Three Tree Point in 1941 from Chicago. Babe died in 1978 and Joe in 1981, but their children, grandchildren, and great-grandchildren still live at Three Tree Point. Joe and his brother Bob had a barbershop in Burien and then at Five Corners, a shopping center east of Three Tree Point. For a time, it seemed like they were the only barbers in town. As can be seen by this picture, the Manolas were a happy, kind, and fun-loving couple. (Kathy and Todd Anderson.)

Both Joe and Babe Manola were in vaudeville before moving to Three Tree Point. In this 1930 photograph, Eddie ? and Joe Manola (right) are performing the act they called The La Salice Brothers in New York. Eddie and Joe were an adagio dancing duo. While traveling the vaudeville circuit, Joe met and later married Babe. (Kathy and Todd Anderson.)

The Three Tree Point Garden Club was founded in 1928 by Mrs. T. C. Smith, and the club continues as an active organization today. The first officers were Mrs. Smith, Mrs. D. Smallwood, Mrs. E. Higgins, and Mrs. R. McGillvray. The mission statement for the club is as follows: "The Three Tree Point Garden Club members enjoy a special bond of common interest and friendship. Gardening is the common interest and enduring attention and concern for each other seals the bond." (Three Tree Point Garden Club.)

These three ladies are celebrating a happy occasion. They are, from left to right, Mrs. Alexander B. Heppler, Mrs. Edward Lincoln Smith, and Mrs. Gilbert L. Duffy Sr. There are 40 candles on the cake, and they may have been celebrating the 40th anniversary of the Three Tree Point Garden Club, founded in 1928. (Wende Duffy.)

These two ladies at the Three Tree Point garden party are looking very fashionable on the lawn of the Rabel home in the 1940s. (Three Tree Point Garden Club.)

In 1946, these Three Tree Point ladies are posing for a snapshot in the garden. They may be members of the garden club or a church organization. They are, from left to right, unidentified, Mrs. McEwan, Moss, Durand, Puckett, Hazel Puckett, unidentified, Bennett, Frazier, Myrtle Harper, and Westley.

The Three Tree Point Garden Club members are enjoying afternoon tea on the grounds of the Rabel home. This home and garden is on the bluff looking south with a beautiful view of Mount Rainier and south Puget Sound. The date isn't shown on the photograph, but it is probably in the 1940s. (Three Tree Point Garden Club)

In 1938, Art Pearson signed on as a salesman for the Fuller Brush Company, and he is still on the job, giving him the distinction of being their longest-serving salesperson ever. Art regularly calls on the housewives of Three Tree Point. In this photograph, he is holding a model of the M. S. *Pearsondam* given to him by the Holland America Line for logging over 250,000 miles and 1,000 cruising days with the cruise line. (Ken Pearson.)

Judie Radinsky (left) and Nancy Smallwood were the best of friends, as can be seen in this photograph taken in 1950. Generations of children have run barefoot on the beach. When school was out, the shoes came off and weren't put back on again until school started in September. The Radinsky girls and the Smallwoods have remained friends all of their lives and share so many fond memories and amusing stories about their beach playground.

Nancy Jordan (left) and Jeannette Manola are sunbathing on the ramp in front of the Manola house in 1953. In those days, baby oil was used for tanning, sometimes with iodine for more color. Cocoa butter was popular too, but neither one offered any protection. When Jeannette married, she and her husband built a house on the corner of 172nd Street and Maplewild Avenue. The Kinnears lived there for decades, and now their daughter lives next door. (Kathy and Todd Anderson.)

This photograph of Virginia Pearce and her cat Jennifer was taken in 1970 at Burien Books, a store that she operated for almost 50 years. Before opening the bookstore, she ran a lending library out of the Three Tree Point Store. Virginia's home was on 172nd Street, where she lived from 1920 until she passed away in 2009. As children, she and her siblings spent all their time on the beach. They had several boats and every year built a raft with a diving board. (Virginia Pearce.)

Ralph Burkhard was a well known architect in the community. He designed buildings at Highline College, Foster Junior-Senior High School, and Washington State University. He was the first to use Glu-laminated beams, corrugated thin shell roofs, and cable suspended walls and roof plates. Ralph's wife, Inez, worked with him by designing the interiors of the buildings. Inez was also an avid skier and one of the founders of the Burien Backsliders Ski Club. (Tor Burkhard.)

Portus Baxter (1867–1962) was a well known and much loved character who lived most of his life at Three Tree Point. He was the sports editor of the *Seattle Post Intelligencer* until he retired in the early 1920s. During his retirement, he lived on 170th Street, just two houses up from the store. Neighbors, and especially children, loved to visit him because he would tell stories for hours. His desk was piled high with papers, and he wrote to everyone. His friends made sure that he attended every athletic event in Seattle, but they wouldn't let him drive after his brakes failed and he ran into the store. (Frank Anderson; Seattle Post-Intelligencer Collection of the Museum of History and Industry.)

On the night of December 17, 1974, Lonnie and Beau Miller's new house burned to the ground. It was located between Beau's parents' home and his grandparents' home. They hadn't yet moved into the house, and it was deemed a no-fault electrical fire. (Lonnie Miller.)

On October 11, 1974, Jerry Gay, staff photographer for the *Seattle Times*, took this Pulitzer Prize–winning photograph of four exhausted firemen resting after battling a house fire at Three Tree Point. The firemen are, from left to right, Joe Guild, Tom Gudmestad, Chris Kitterman, and Jim Flick. The John Neuffer family escaped unharmed after the fire broke out at 3:00 a.m. They were awakened by the barking of a stray dog that they had adopted. The house was on a steep bank and difficult for the firemen to reach with their hoses. (Jerry Gay; *The Seattle Times*.)

The belted kingfisher perches on a branch, and when it spies a fish it flies from the tree and hovers over the water before plunging straight down for its prey. The kingfisher lays its eggs at the end of a long tunnel in a bank. The birds don't build nests; instead, regurgitated fish bones build up under the eggs by the time they hatch. (Ethan Janson.)

Rachel the raccoon became a house pet for Phil Fleming after her mother was killed by a combine in eastern Washington. Rachel routinely went with Phil on his single rowing shell as he rowed around Three Tree Point. He couldn't row too fast or Rachel would get seasick. She would go out prowling every night from 1:00 a.m. to 4:00 a.m. and occasionally had run-ins with neighbors when she wandered into their houses through the cat door. (Phil Fleming.)

The navigation buoy off of Three Tree Point provides a safe resting place for this California sea lion, who is taking a mid-afternoon nap. The male California sea lion can reach as much as 1,000 pounds, and their only natural predators in Puget Sound are orcas (killer whales). The noisy barking from this buoy can be heard all over the neighborhood. These animals are protected by the Marine Mammal Protection Act. (Doug Shadel.)

A Southern Resident killer whale frolics in the waters off of Three Tree Point. The J Pod Southern Residents make regular journeys past Three Tree Point on their way to south Puget Sound. On October 22, 2009, Renee and Emily Shadel spotted a pod of nine killer whales being followed by NOAA scientists who were studying the whales' dietary patterns. (Jeff Hogan—Killer Whale Tales.)

Bald eagles usually avoid human activity, but at Three Tree Point they are a very common sight. In the picture above, two eaglets cry out for nourishment as they sit high atop a dead tree near Three Tree Point. The females lay one to three eggs in a large nest of sticks, usually in tall trees. They primarily feed on fish but will eat rodents and domestic cats. In the picture below, a mature bald eagle is on the prowl for fish along the south beach. These birds are 30 to 43 inches long and have a wingspan of 78 to 96 inches. Their voices create a thin, chattering sound, quite unsuitable to the majesty of this national symbol. Since chemicals such as DDT were banned in the early 1970s, eagles have made a comeback and are no longer endangered but are classified as threatened by the federal government. (Both Ethan Janson.)

Evening falls on the majestic landscape of Three Tree Point under the watchful eye of a setting sun. (Ethan Janson.)

Visit us at
arcadiapublishing.com